MORE SNOOPY COLLECTIBLES:

AN UNAUTHORIZED GUIDE

JAN LINDENBERGER

© 1958,1965 United Feature Syndicate Inc.

Schiffer Publishing Ltd

4880 Lower Valley Road, Atglen, PA 19310 USA

ACKNOWLEDGMENTS

I wish to give a very special thank you to Cher Porges and her family. Without Cher the Snoopy books would not have been possible. We worked many weeks and long hours to give this project the value it deserves. Her patience in arranging and rearranging her vast collection was greatly appreciated. In the process she says that she found things she had forgotten were there. The information for this price guide came from her years of knowledge and research.

Between diet sodas and mustard pretzels and the privilege of me sleeping near "The Snoopy room", *The Unauthorized Guide to Snoopy Collectibles* and this book, *More Snoopy Collectibles: An Unauthorized Guide*, were born.

Together we worked hard to provide much needed, all color information and price guides to Snoopy collectibles. So again I thank Cher. It was wonderful working with you and I have gained you and your family as my valued friends. That's the best part of this job.

Thanks also to Laurel Sherry from New Holstein, Wisconsin. Laurel is the show promotor for the Mid West Snoopy Swap Meet. She allowed me to photograph on show and encouraged me to do this book. Thanks too, to all the dealers at the show that let me photograph their Snoopy's. For information about the Snoopy swap meet contact Laurel by phone or fax at 414-898-5578.

Nancy Wilke, Chesterfield, Missouri, gave Cher and I a day's worth of hard work and spent many hours on the phone with Cher giving us valuable information. Thanks, Nancy. Thanks also to: Warren Chamberlin, Mishawauka, Indiana; Kevin Knauer, Colorado Springs, Colorado; and Joel Martone, Colorado Springs, Colorado.

Published by Schiffer Publishing, Ltd.
4880 Lower Valley Road
Atglen, PA 19310
Phone: (610) 593-1777
Fax: (610) 593-2002
E-mail:Schifferbk@aol.com
Please write for a free catalog.
This book may be purchased from the publisher.
Please include $2.95 for shipping.
Try your bookstore first.

We are interested in hearing from authors
with book ideas on related subjects.

DESIGNED BY BONNIE M. HENSLEY

CONTENTS

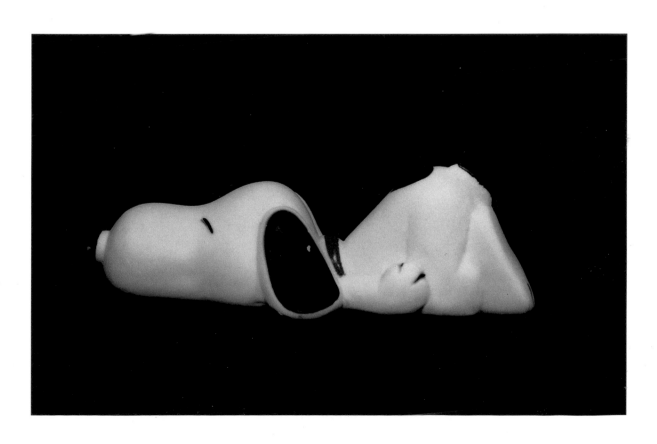

INTRODUCTION

Welcome to *More Snoopy Collectibles*. Even when I was working on *The Unauthorized Guide to Snoopy Collectibles* I was sure that I would never cover every thing. And, of course, this isn't the entire number or variety of Snoopy collectibles that were ever produced or that are available today. Everyday something new enters the market, so the best I can do is to provide the collector up-to-date and general information and a current price guide for this lovable beagle. Later, I will be writing two additional books on the collectibles of the Peanuts gang, and I am sure that Snoopy will make another appearance there. For now I hope you enjoy "More Snoopy Collectibles."

Snoopy is the creation of Charles Monroe Schulz. Always a lover of cartoons, Schulz was even nicknamed Sparky, after the horse in the Barney Google comics. Schulz pursued cartooning through a "mail order" art school, and then began teaching for the same school. In 1950 he traveled to New York and United Features Syndicate to offer them his "L'il Folks" comic strip. They liked the concept and changed the name to "Peanuts." They also tried to limit the role of the dog, Snoopy. Schulz stood by his guns and Snoopy became the central character of the Peanuts gang.

The love of Snoopy is universal. Around the world people love the characters, and as you will see in this book, the comic strip and the products it has inspired are translated into many languages.

The character of Snoopy has changed immensely over the years. You can tell this by his five different two-dimensional copyright dates. When Snoopy first appeared in 1950 he always walked on four feet or sat on his haunches. This was his earliest copyright date. He earned another copyright in 1956 when he was shown dancing on two feet with his head high. He was walking on two feet all the time by 1958, thus earning his third copyright date. His fourth copyright date came in 1965, with his ears tucked under his aviators hat and goggles covering his eyes, he began his battles as the Flying Ace, fighting his nemesis the Red Baron. His final copyright date came in 1971, when Joe Cool appeared on the scene. Yet through all these changes he kept his lovable personality and his enduring charm.

HINTS FOR COLLECTORS

By far the best place to buy Snoopy Collectibles is the Mid West Snoopy Swap Meet. This show and sale is organized by Laurel Sherry. One may contact Laurel at 1723 Monroe St. New Holstein, Wisconsin. 53061 for information on the next meet. Phone/fax 414-898-5578.

Several hundred people who love Snoopy get together to buy, sell, trade and talk Snoopy. You will find Snoopy and the Peanuts Gang in abundance. The prices are more than fair and the spirit among the sellers is very cheerful. To the collector, it's better than Christmas. You can tell they all love that beagle!

Searching for Snoopy is fun and challenging. While waiting for the Snoopy Swap Meet, a good way to start a collection is to scour garage sales and flea markets. The prices are usually negotiable but the merchandise isn't always mint. The more flaws the less you should have to pay.

Antique Malls can also be fruitful. Prices vary extremely but, depending on condition and how knowledgeable the seller is, merchandise can be reasonably had.

If the item catches your eye and you must have it, it's quite convenient to purchase it at the mall or antique shop. Remember the old slogan, 'You snooze, you loose?" Purchase it when you see it or it may not be there when you go back.

If you have a bit more cash, toy shows are wonderful. Prices can be negotiated slightly and merchandise is generally in good condition. There are also several toy magazines which have advertisements from all over the country. This is a good way to track down hard-to-find treasures.

For new items a good source, especially around the holiday season when special things come on the market, is Knotts Berry Farms, Camp Snoopy.

Whatever path you choose to take in your search for Snoopy, remember the real search is for fun!

I hope you enjoy this Snoopy collectibles guide. Prices may vary according to area, availability, and condition. Please take this book with you on your "Snoopy search" and happy hunting!

SNOOPY: © 1956 United Feature Syndicate, Inc.

BIBLIOGRAPHY

Johnson, Rheta Grinslay. *Good Grief: The Story of Charles Schulz.* New York: Pharos Books, 1989. Pharos Book. New York.

Fanning, Jim. *Boomer Magazine,* April, 1995. Dubuque, Iowa: Antique Trader Publicatons. Dubuque, Iowa.

Holt, Charles M. *You Don't Look 35 Charlie Brown.* New York: Holt, Rinehart, Winston, 35.

LIVING WITH SNOOPY

TROPHIES

Aviva trophies total well over 100. They were produced in large quantities throughout the 1970s and into the 1980s. While they portrayed the entire Peanuts gang, Snoopy and Woodstock were the most represented. Snoopy being the most common, unless unusual, $8-10. Variations include a larger scenic trophy, early 1970s, $15-20. Sparkies were mounted on teakwood base without message. 1971/1972, $25-35.

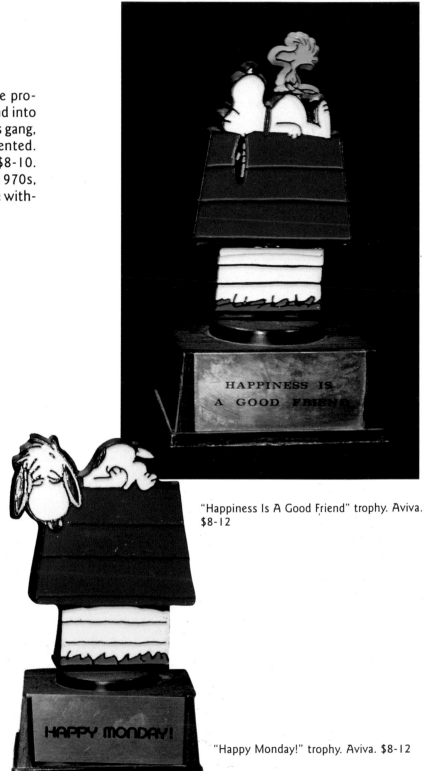

"Happiness Is A Good Friend" trophy. Aviva. $8-12

"America You're Beautiful" trophy. Aviva. $12-18

"Happy Monday!" trophy. Aviva. $8-12

"World's Best Driver" trophy. Aviva. $8-12

"World's Biggest Clown" trophy. Aviva. $8-12

"World's Greatest Bowler" trophy from Aviva.
1970s-80s. $8-12

"World's Greatest Tennis
Player" trophy. Aviva.
$8-12

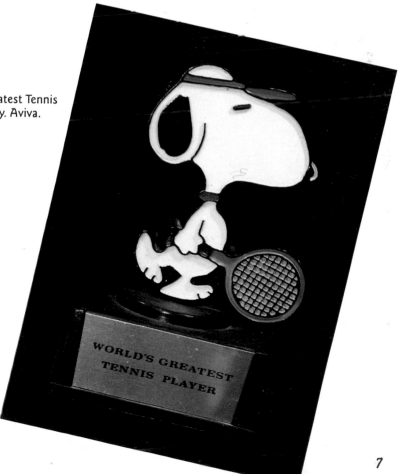

"World's Greatest Golfer" trophy from Aviva. 1970s-80s. $8-12.

"You're the Joe Coolest" trophy. Aviva. $8-12

"Happiness is you and me" trophy. Aviva. $8-12

"Joe Rembrandt" trophy. Aviva. $8-12

"Think Snow" trophy. Aviva. $8-12

"You're A Real Winner" trophy. Aviva. $8-12

Santa Snoopy trophy in box. Aviva. 1980s. $18-25

Plastic Snoopy NFL trophy. Mid-1980s. 28 different team trophies were produced. Made by Quantasia. $15-20

Scenic trophy, plastic Snoopy, the skier. $18-25

Scenic trophy, plastic cupid Snoopy with Woodstock. $18-25

Wall plaque, Snoopy dancing with Woodstock from Hallmark. 3" x 4.5". 1970s. $5-7

"The grade A teacher award." Hallmark. 1980s. $5-7

Hallmark wall plaque, Snoopy with friend Woodstock. 6" x 6". 1970s. $8-12

Wall plaque. "Happy Today." Hallmark. 3" x 4.5". 1970s. $5-7

Round wall plaque. "Merry Christmas Teacher." 1982. Hallmark. 3" x 4.5". $6-8

Hallmark wall plaque, Snoopy hugging Woodstock. 7" x 7". 1980s. $8-12

Hallmark wall plaque, Snoopy bringing a flower to Woodstock. 5" x 7". 1980s. $8-12

Mirror, Snoopy and Woodstock, wood frame. Determined. England. 8" x 10". 1970s. $30-40

Hallmark wall plaque, Snoopy with trophy and Woodstock. 3" x 4.5". 1990s. $5-7

Mirror, "I think I'm alergic to morning!" Wood frame. Determined. England. 8" x 10". 1970s. $30-40

Snoopy enamel on metal, picture frames from Butterfly. 1979. $15-20.

Mirror, "Who's the coolest of them all?" Plastic frame by Determined. 8" x 10". 1980s. $15-20

Picture holder from Butterfly. Opens like a compact. Late 1970s. $20-30

Metal enamel heart-shaped Snoopy frame by Butterfly. 1979. $20-30

Snoopy metal picture frames. 1980s. $15-20

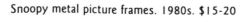

Production cel from Saturday morning cartoon series, the "Charlie Brown and Snoopy Show." 1980s. Framed, double matted.
$500-600

"Let the good times roll!" Plastic picture frame. 1980s. $10-15

Joe Ranger picture frame with package. 1980s. $12-15

Stained glass Snoopy ornament from Oden. 1980. 5.5", $35-45. 3.5", $30-40. Not shown: Snoopy howling at a crescent moon, $45-55; Snoopy dancing, $25-35; Snoopy sitting, 5.5": $25-35, 4.75": $20-30; Joe Cool, 4.5", $25-35; Snoopy with yellow parachute, 8.5", $40-50; Snoopy laying on red heart, $35-45; Snoopy sitting with Woodstock, $35-45; Flying Ace, $35-45; Snoopy on doghouse with Woodstock on his tummy, 6.75", $40-50; Snoopy sits next to supper dish with Woodstock in dish, $35-45.

Leaded glass Snoopy window, Hand made by Clayton Anderson, Andy Crafts. 1980s. $600-750

Snoopy-Joe Cool sunshiner from Aviva. Late 1970s. $15-20

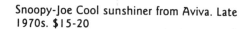

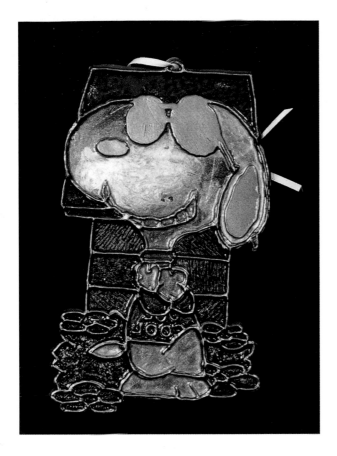

Needle point Snoopy on skis. Malina. Late 1970s. $10-15 each

Joe Cool painted window hanging stained glass illusion. 5" x 7". Aviva. 1981. $25-35. Not shown: Flying Ace, Joe Gourmet, Snoopy and Woodstock with balloons. $25-35 each

Embroidered Snoopy wall set. Color stitch kits for kids, completed. JCA, late 1980s-1990s. $10-15 each

Embroidered Snoopy wall set. Color stitch kits for kids, completed. JCA, late 1980s-1990s. $10-15

Color stitch kit for kids, late 1980s. JCA, Inc. $10-15.

Snoopy reading paper, cork bulletin board. Manton Cork Corp. 1980s. $15-25

Snoopy on stick horse, cork bulletin board. Manton Cork Corp. 1980s. $15-25

Cork bulletin board. Manton Cork corp. 1980s. $15-25

Felt Snoopy banner. 1970s.
Determined Products.
$15-25

Peanuts Fall Decorations from Hallmark. Late
1980s early 1990s. $4-7

Peanuts Football Press-out Decorations.
Hallmark. 1970s. $15-20

Felt Flying Ace banner.
1970s. Determined
Products. $15-25

Felt banners. Determined Products. 1970s. $15-25

Felt Snoopy and Woodstock banner. 1970s. Determined Products. $15-25

Felt Snoopy banner. 1970s. Determined Products. $15-25

Felt banner. "Snoopy for President." Determined. 1970s. $15-20

Linen towel. "Snoopy for Prime Minister." 20" x 30". 1980s. Made in United Kingdom. $25-35

Felt calendar. 1983. Bucilla kit, jeweled. $25-35

Nylon embroidered Snoopy on doghouse flag.
NCE, 1995. $20-25

Mylar banners. Mid-1990s. 34.75" x 5". $3-4

Plastic door knockers. Butterfly. Late 1970s.
$7-14

Nylon screen printed Joe Cool flag. NCE 1996.
$10-15

FLOOR STUFF

Peanuts Latch Hook Kit. Came with rug inside.
Malina, 1970s. $35-45

Latch hook Christmas rug of Snoopy and
Woodstock from Malina, made from a kit.
1970s. $35-45

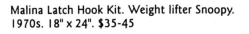

Malina Latch Hook Kit. Weight lifter Snoopy.
1970s. 18" x 24". $35-45

Latch hook Snoopy in suit, rug from Malina Co. Made from kit.
1980s. $35-45

Latch hook Snoopy jogging rug from Malina Co. Made from a kit. 1980s. $35-45

Cotton weave throw rug. Do not disturb Snoopy. $15-25

In the 1990s, Frank T. Greco Inc. produced a large, reasonably priced selection of cotton throw rugs that could be utiized for floor or wall decoration. These high quality handmade and individually screen printed rugs came in various sizes with different scenes depicted. 22" x 40". 20" x 34".

Cotton weave throw rug. Flying Ace. $15-25

Cotton weave throw rug. Snoopy in sports car. $15-25

Cotton weave throw rug. Snoopy with train. $15-25

Rubber "Happy Holidays" door mat.
1980-90s. $25-35

Rubber personialized door mat.
1980s. $25-35

Welcome mat, indoor or outdoor. Bacova Guild
Ltd. Olefin carpets. 1990s. $10-15

Welcome mat, Snoopy and Woodstock. Bacova
Guild Ltd. Olefin carpets. 1990s. $10-15

Acrylic plush Snoopy cowboy, rug. 1990s.
$15-20

BOOK STUFF

Ceramic pair of Snoopy bookends. $40-50

Ceramic Snoopy sitting bookends. $30-40

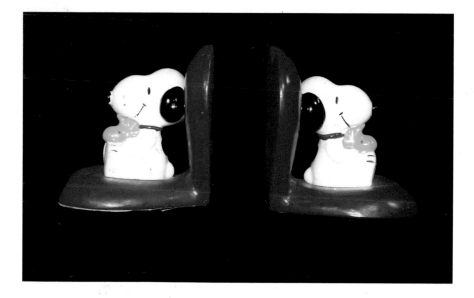

Rubber bookends. Woodstock and Snoopy on heart shaped base.
Butterfly, 1981. $25-35

Ceramic train bookends. Willitts. 1990. $40-50

OUTDOOR STUFF

Snoopy giant thermometer by Sybron/Taylor.
11" x 12" 1979. $50-75 with box

Bird feeder featuring Snoopy on dog house with Woodstock on
the perch. Con Agri Inc. Early 1980s. $25-35

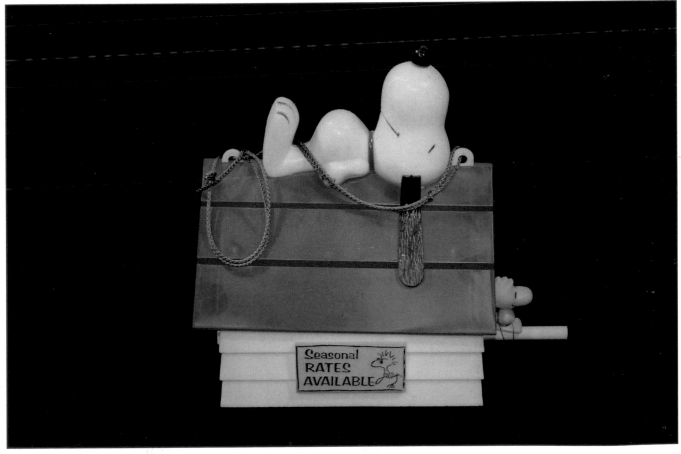

LIFE IS FOR THE DOGS!

"Fetching Cologne for Precious Pets." Snoopy Private Collection. "A rugged, spicy scent." $10-15

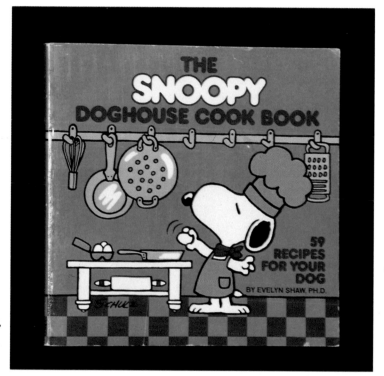

The Snoopy Doghouse Cookbook. Evelyn Shaw, PH.D. 1980s. $12-18

Plastic Snoopy dishes. Determined. Early 1970s. 5". $10-20

Plastic Snoopy dog dish by Determined. Came in a varity of colors and 5" and 7" sizes. 1970s. $10-20

Plastic Snoopy dog dish by Determined. Came in a variety of colors and 5" and 7" sizes. 1970s. $10-20

Ceramic dog dish. A bone sits inside. 1994. Benjamin and Medwin. $25-35

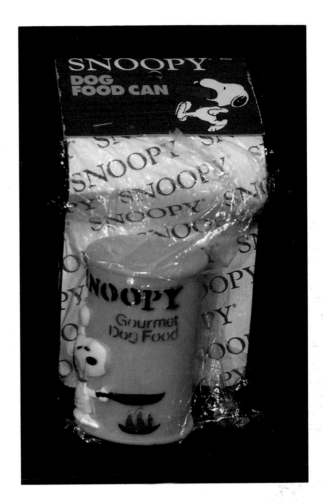

Rubber dog food can, squeaking dog toy from Conagra Pet Products. 1980s-90s. $4-6

Snoopy surrounded by a Christmas wreath, squeaking vinyl dog toy. Con Agra, 1980s-1990s. $4-6

Snoopy plastic feeding dog mat. 1990s. $6-8

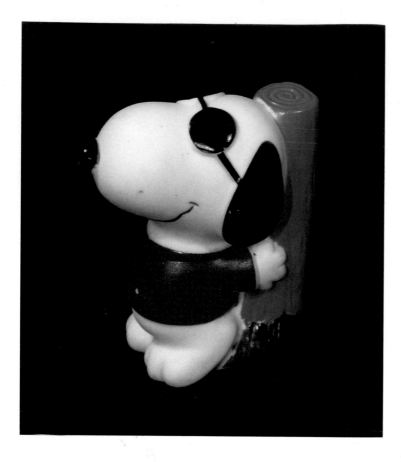

Joe Cool squeaking vinyl dog toy. Con Agra, 1980s-90s.. $4-6

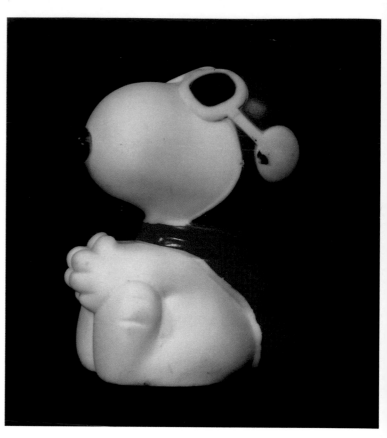

Flying Ace squeaking dog toy from Conagra Pet Products. 1980s and 1990s. $4-6

Jogging Snoopy squeeking vinyl dog or baby toy. Danara. 1980s. $5-8

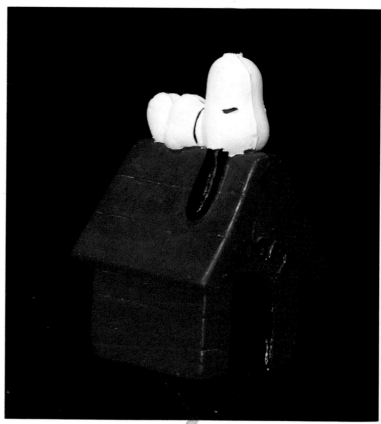

Snoopy on house squeaking dog toy from Conagra Pet Products. 1980s-90s. $4-6

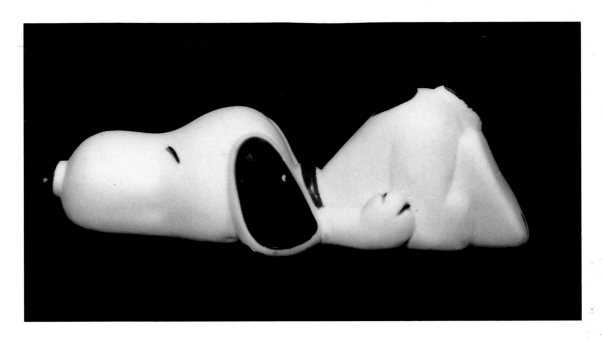

Rubber Snoopy squeaking dog toy from Conagra Pet Products.
1980s-90s. $4-6

Rubber shoe squeaking dog toy from Conagra Pet Products.
1980s-90s. $4-6

Rubber newspaper squeaking dog toy from Conagra Pet Products.
1980s-90s. $4-6

SNOOPY'S SCHOOLTIME

PAPER STUFF

Advertising poster for education. 1990s. $5-7

Gymnast Snoopy, ring binder. 1970s. $8-12

Notebook ring binder with Snoopy and Woodstock. Early 1980s.
$8-12

Paper note pads. 1980s-90s. $2-3 each

Snoopy score pad. Hallmark. Complete playing card ensemble came with box, two decks of matching cards, score pad, and a mechanical pencil. Mid-1970s. $35-45

Snoopy climbing rock notebook. 1980s. $8-12

Snoopy and Woodstock ring binder. 1970s. $8-12.

Scratch pads. Hallmark. Snoopy,1980s, $8-11. Sally, 1990s, $5-6

Snoopy cover booklet of note cards. Hallmark. 1970s. Complete notebook, $15-20

Snoopy friend to friend note cards. One of many in booklet.

Snoopy note cards. One of a booklet.

Peanuts gang autograph book. Butterfly. 1980s. $5-7

Peanuts gangs mini-memo pads. Butterfly. 1980s. $5-7 each

Woodstock pocket notebook. Butterfly. 1980s. $5-7

UltimateMemo, magnetic and wipe off board from Manton. 1980s.
$12-15

Vinyl Peanuts Roll Call, a mini clip notebook
from Butterfly. 1980s. $5-7

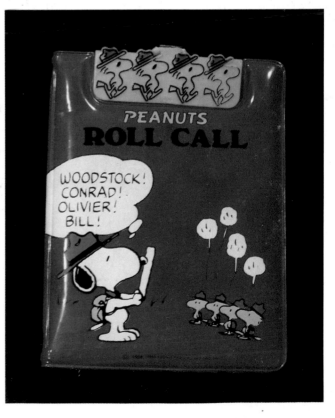

Snoopys mini note pad and pad and pencil set. Butterfly. 1980s.
$5-7 each

Plastic covered mini address book. Butterfly. 1980s. $4-6

Mini notes. Butterfly. 1980s. $4-6

Plastic "Snoopy Mini Pencil Pal Telephone Book." Butterfly mini. 1980s. $5-7

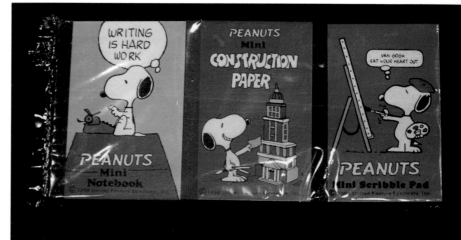

Mini Peanuts paper set. Butterfly. 1980s. $6-8

"Plastic Wipe Off" note board. Butterfly. 1980s. $5-7

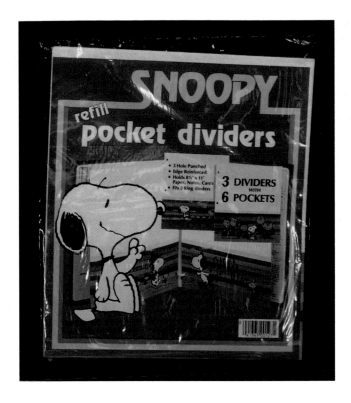

"Snoopy Pocket Dividers." Plymouth Inc. manufactured for Butterfly. 1980s. $6-8

Boxed mini-stationary with envelopes. Hallmark. 1990s. $15-20

Snoopy boxed stationary. Hallmark. 1980s. Mint/boxed, complete with envelopes. $15-20 set

"Peanuts Letter Set. Butterfy mini. 1980s. $5-7

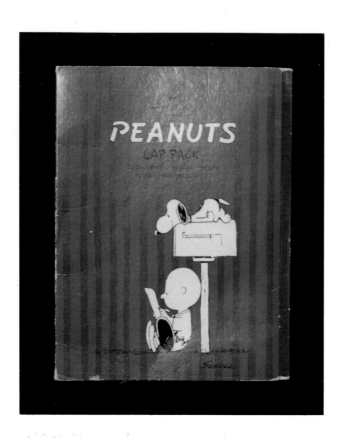

"Peanuts Lap Pack." Note paper, envelopes. Hallmark, 1970s. $15-20 complete

Laminated book cover. Plymouth Inc. Manufactured for Butterfly. 1980s. $4-6

WRITING STUFF

Snoopy boxes of crayons. Butterfly. 1980s. $5-7

Plastic Snoopy pencil holders filled with colored pencils or regular pencils. Empire Berol, 1990s. $5-8

Set of 12 color pencils. Empire Berol Co. 1980s
$5-7

Gold Snoopy gold-filled pen in tin case. Stylus.
1995. $25-30

Snoopy pen and pencil sets. Empire/Empire Berol. 1980s-90s. $3-6
set

"Peanuts Pens." 6 pack of Snoopy pens. $16-19. 4 pack of party
pens, Peanuts gang. $10-12

Plastic pencil cases. Hallmark, early 1980s. $8-12

Snoopy "Mini Pencil Set." Butterfly. 1980s. $5-7

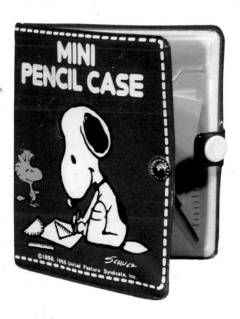

Plastic "Mini Pencil Case." Butterfly. 1980s. $4-6

Tin Snoopy heart-shaped box. Filled with rubber stamp and ink etc. Japan. Butterfly. 1980s. $15-20

WHAT DAY IS THIS?

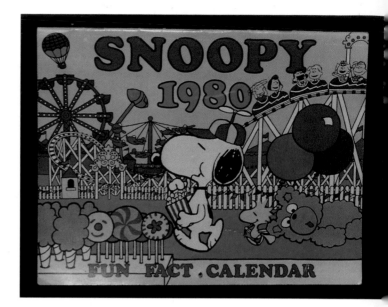

Snoopy 1980 calendar. $18-22

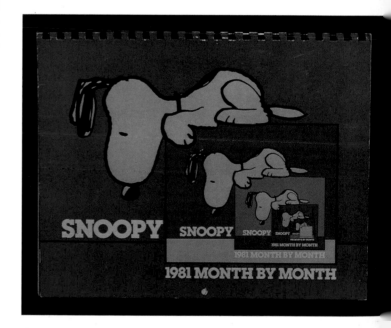

"Snoopy 1981 Monthly Calendar." 1980. $18-22

Opposite Page
Top left: "Snoopy 1992 Calendar." $10-15
Center left: Snoopy and Woodstock sticker calendar. Ambassador. 1995. $8-10
Bottom left: Hallmark Peanuts desk calendar. 1995. $15-20

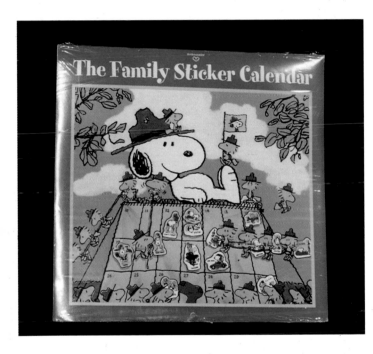

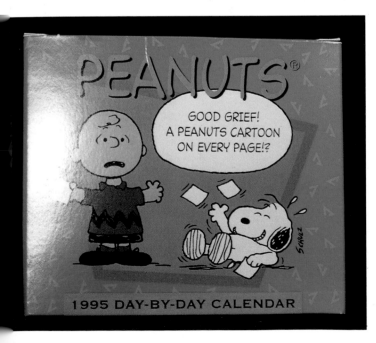

Plastic school supplies. Pen holder and book mark. Butterfly. 1980s. $5-7 each

Plastic paper clip in the shape of a cloths pin. Butterfly. 1980s. $3-5

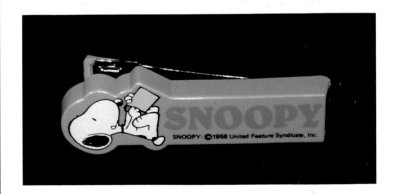

Plastic Snoopy stapler. Butterfly. 1980s. $7-9

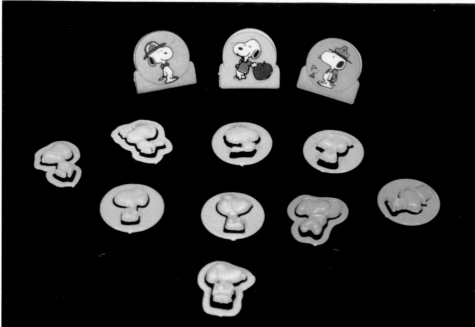

Snoopy office supplies. Tape dispenser or glue. Butterfly. 1980s. $5-7 each

Plastic paper clips featuring the Peanuts gang. Mini clamps sold in packages as a set. Paper clips sold as a set also. 1980s. $6-8 set

Rubber stamper kits. The Rubber Stamp Factory. 1990s. $7-15

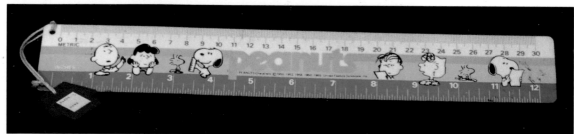

Plastic ruler. Snoopy and friends. 1980s. $3-5

Plastic Peanuts gang ruler. Butterfly. 1980s. $4-6

Plastic pencils/pen holders. 1990s. $6-10

Plastic pencil sharpener. Maker unknown. Late 1980s. $20-30

Stick on looseleaf reinforcements. Butterfly.1980s. $4-6

Plastic paper clips from Japan. 1990s. $5-7

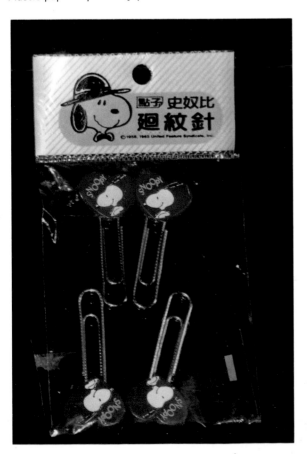

Snoopy on doghouse pencil sharpener. Kenner. Battery operated. 1974. $45-60 in box

Refrigerator magnets. Wecolite. 1980s-90s. $3-5 per card

Magnets. Magnetic Collectibles Ltd. 1990s. $3-4 each. Also available in shrink wrapped package.

Variety of cities refrigerator magnets. Mid-1990s. Magnetic Collectibles Ltd. $3-4 each

Variety of cities refrigerator magnets. Mid-1990s. Magnetic Collectibles Ltd. $3-4 each

Variety of Christmas refrigerator magnets. Mid-1990s. Magnetic Collectibles Inc. $3-4 each

Variety of sports refrigerator magnets. Mid-1990s. Magnetic Collectibles Ltd. $3-4 each

Plastic "Snoopy Play Smock." Empire Pencil. 1980s. $7-10

Magnetic bulletin board containing Snoopy magnets of various materials. Ceramic, vinyl, rubber and plastic. 1980-1990s. $3-8 each.

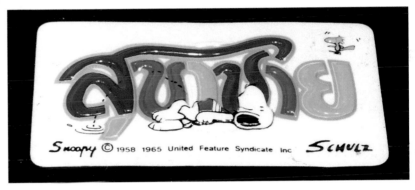

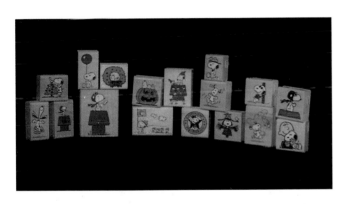

Japanese vinyl sticker. 4.5" x 2.5". 1990s. $5-7

Wooden rubber stamps. Rubber Stampede depending on size. 1980s. $6-15

Canon calculator and instructions. 1980s. $25-30

WHAT'S FOR LUNCH?

Plastic Snoopy lunch box, King Seeley Thermos. 1980s. $15-20

Cardboard lunch box, Snoopy's doghouse. Dolly Madison promotion. 1970s. $10-12

Metal Peanuts lunch box, King Seeley Thermos. 1980s. $20-30

Nylon Snoopy lunch tote with King Seeley Thermos. Mid-1990s. $15-20

Plastic Snoopy lunch box, King Seeley Thermos. 1980s. $15-20

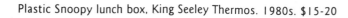

Metal Snoopy lunch box, King Seeley Thermos. Late 1960s.
$30-40

Metal lunch box. Snoopy and Woodstock on swing. Japan. 1990s. $20-30

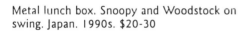

Nylon insulated tote. 1980s. $15-20

Plastic flashing key chains. Hallmark. Early 1970s. $15-20

Brass "Ski," Snoopy key chain. Quantasia. 1980s. $7-10

Plastic "Snoopy Fan Club," key chain. Quantasia. 1980s. $6-8

Plastic Flying Ace key chain. Made exclusively for Knotts Berry Farms by Brabo Group. 1990s. $3-4

Plastic square Snoopy and Woodstock key chain. 1980s. Aviva. $5-7

Plastic Snoopy and Woodstock key chain. Monogram Products. 1990s. $4-6

Joe Cool, rubber key chain. Accessory Network. Mid-1990s. $4-6

Plastic Snoopy, initial key chain. 1990s. Monogram Products. $4-6

Plastic airplane key chain. Japan. 1990s. $5-7

Plastic snowman and Snoopy key chain. Quantasia. 1980s. $6-8

Plastic skating Snoopy key chain. Monogram Products. 1990s. $4-6

Snoopy key chain. Applause. 1990s. $4-6

SNOOPY'S LIBRARY

READ TO ME!

Peanuts, 1952 and Snoopy, 1958 by Charles Schulz. Paperback. Rinehart & Co. Inc. $3-15 depending on condition and edition

Snoopy greeting card. 1980s. $3-4

The Gospel According to Peanuts by Robert L. Shorts. John Knox Press. 1965. Paperback $8-12. Hardback $20-25

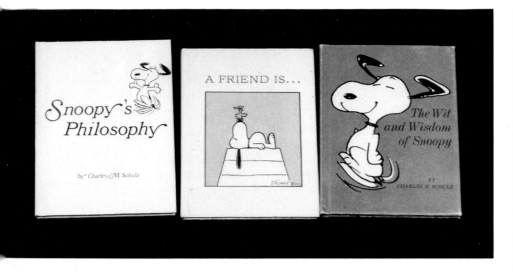

3 Snoopy books by Charles Schulz from Hallmark. Each book is part of a different set. *Peanut Philsophy*, 1972. Other books in this set but not shown are *Linus on Life*, *The Wisdom of Charlie Brown*, and *The World According to Lucy*. They came in a cardboard case. $30-35 set or $6-8 each. *More Peanuts Philosophy* was also issued in 1972. *A Friend Is...*, 1972. $6-8. Other books in this set were *All About Birthdays*, 1971, $7-9 and *All About Friendship*, 1968, $8-10. *The Wit and Wisdom of Snoopy* was part of set including *Lucy Looks at Life*, *Charlie Brown's Reflections*, and *The Meditations of Linus*. They came in a cardboard case. $30-35 set or $6-8 each. Thoughtfulness Library.

Snoopy: Everyone's Favorite Beagle Since 1950, by Charles M. Schulz, an anniversary book. $40-50

Snoopy and "It Was a Dark and Stormy Night" story book by Charles M. Schulz. Hardback with dust cover. Holt, Rinehart & Winston. Early 1970s. $12-18

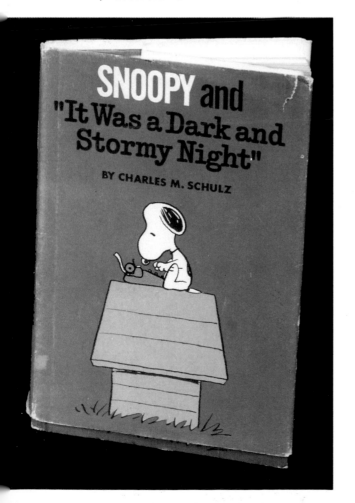

"I Never Promised You an Apple Orchard" The Collected Writings of Snoopy by Charles M. Schulz. Hardback with dust cover, story book. Holt, Rinehart & Winston. 1976. $12-18

The World of Charlie Brown. "A Mattel Book Set." 1980s. $30-40

Charles M. Schulz: 40 Years of life and Art, by Giovanni Trinboli. Pharos Books, New York, printed in Italy. 1990. $100-125 mint in box

The Snoopy Collection: One Thousand Fabulous Snoopy Products. Edited by J.C. Saures. 1982. Hardback $30-40; paperback $15-20

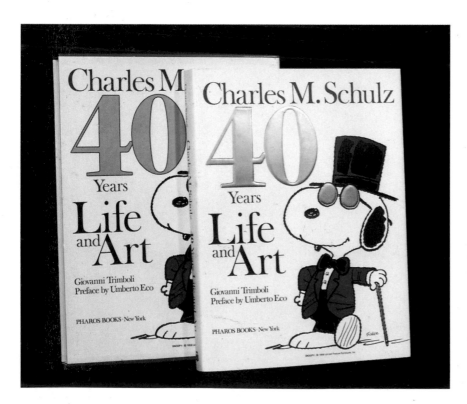

Snoopy Around the World: Dressed by Top Fashion Designers. Published by Harry Abrams, Inc. 1990. $40-50

Snoopy Et La S' Valentin.
French. Dargaud. $12-18

Incroyable Snoopy.
French book.
Dargaud. $12-18

The Snoopy Festival, by Charles M. Schulz. Holt, Rinehart &
Winston. 1974. Paperback $15-20. Hardback $30-40

Snoopy, Come Home by Charles M. Schulz in English and Spanish
versions. Holt, Rinehart & Winston Publishers. 1960s. $25-30
together.

Snoopy coloring book from Kuwait. Mid-1990s. $9-11

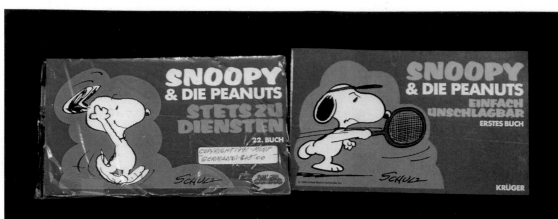

Snoopy books in German. Paperback. Kruger. 1990s. $14-18

Snoopy Patineur. French book. Dargaud. $12-18

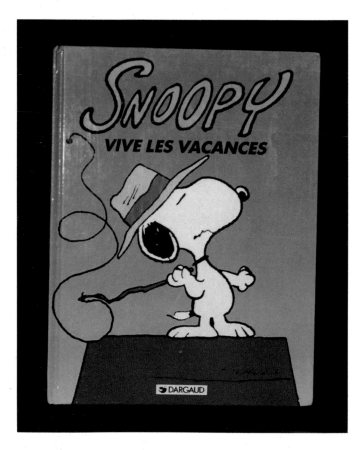

Snoopy Vive Les Vacances. French hardback book. Dargaud. 1990s. $20-25

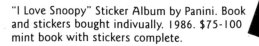

"I Love Snoopy" Sticker Album by Panini. Book and stickers bought indivually. 1986. $75-100 mint book with stickers complete.

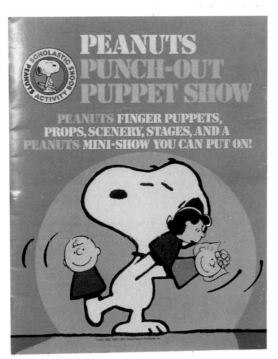

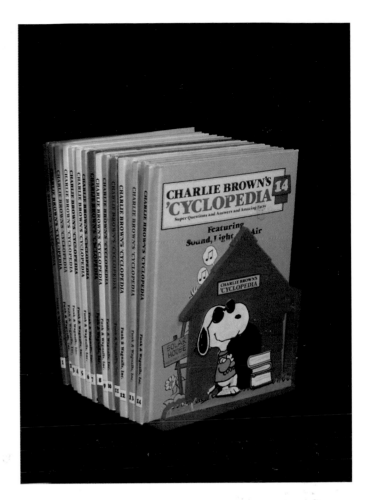

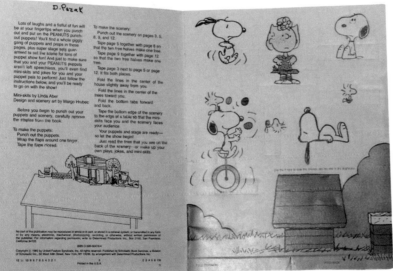

Charlie Brown's 'Cyclopedia with rack. Funk and Wagnalls. 1990s. $30-35 set with rack. 14 volumes

Peanuts Punch-out Puppet Show. Scholastic. 1980s. $10-15

STUFF TO DO

Gift pack. Book, cotton Snoopy, tote bag. Applause. Late 1980s. $15-20

"Box of Coloring Books." Set of four by Modern Publications. 1980s. $15-20

It's Your Serve, Snoopy Coloring Book. Rand McNally. 1980. $6-8

Snoopy "Posters Pen Set." Craft House Co. 1980s. $10-15

Peanuts, Sound Story musical story book. Sight and Sound Inc. 1989. $20-25

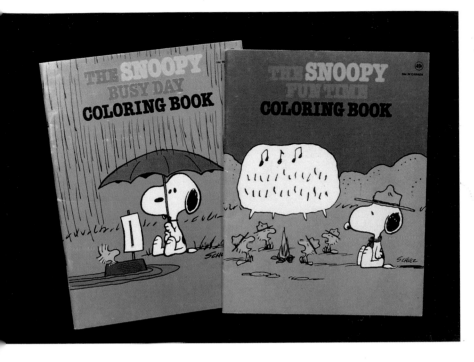

Snoopy "Busy Day" and "Fun Time" coloring books. Ottenheimer Publishers. Early 1980s. $3-5 each

Plastic "Snoopy Book and Toy Set." Random House. 1980s. $9-12

Pet Snoopy story book. Determined. 1983. $10-12 mint

Gift pack. Book, cotton Snoopy, tote bag. Applause. Late 1980s. $15-20

SIGN HERE PLEASE!

Hallmark photo album. 6" x 4.5". 1980s. $12-18

Autograph book with Snoopy carrying hobo pack. Hallmark. Early 1970s. $25-30

"Sign In Please!" Snoopy autograph book. Hallmark. 1990s. $6-8

"No Snooping" diary with lock. Hallmark. Mid-1990s. $10-12

"Super" Snoopy scrapbook. Hallmark. 1990s. $20-30

Small photo album from Knott's Berry Farm. 1980s/1990s. $10-12

Spiral Snoopy and Wood-
stock scrapbook album.
Hallmark. Late 1970s.
$25-30 mint in box

Small photo album with Snoopy puffing hot air
balloon. Japan. Knotts Berry Farm. 1990s.
$10-12

Snoopy photo album.
Japan. Full size. 1990s.
$30-40

The Peanuts gang photo
album. Ambassador. 1995.
$10-15

"The Peanuts Thoughtfulness Album."
Hallmark. Loose leaf folders and calendar. 8" x
10". Early 1970s. $40-50

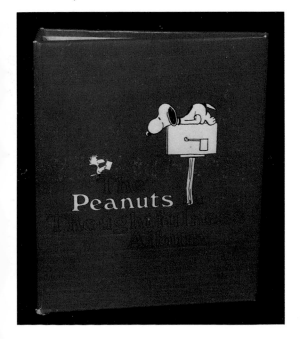

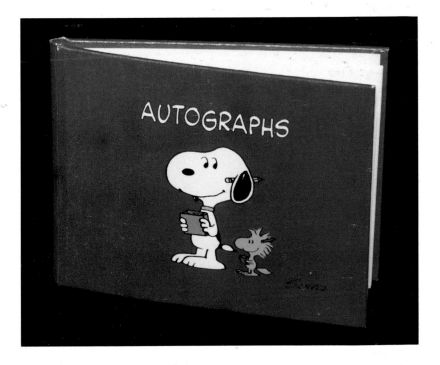

Snoopy autograph book. Hallmark. 1980s. $12-18

PAPER STUFF

Snoopy Fan Club papers. 1983. $7-10 set

Booklet for 1961 Falcon with Snoopy at bottom. $35-45

Japanese advertising for ski resorts. 1990s. $6-8 each

Official program from the 85th Tournament of Roses. 1974.
$15-20

Beagle Bugle newsletter, September, 1983, $15-20. The *Beagle Bugle* newsletter was published quarterly for members of the original Snoopy fan club. General manager, George Pipal and publisher, R.A. Nelson, worked out of Schulz's headquarters, 9 Snoopy Place, Santa Rosa, California. This wonderful paper was first published February, 1983 and included articles about Snoopy and the Gang, advice to pet owners, color photos from fans worldwide, new products and special offers to members for great memorabilia. Mid 1985 saw the end of the newsletter, due to the high costs of color printing and postal costs. Subscription costs were $3 for four newsletters.

Beagle Bugle newsletter. December. 1983. $15-20

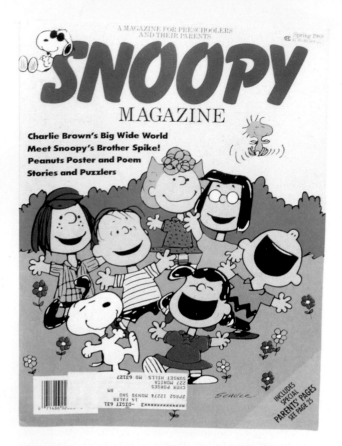

Snoopy Magazine. Summer, 1988. $10-15

Snoopy Magazine, Spring Issue No. 2. 1988. $10-15. Welsh Publishing Group Inc. published Snoopy Magazine quarterly. It included stories, coloring pages, puzzles, riddles and even more great features. Parents could enjoy helpful tips on the parents pages in every issue. The magazine was designed for pre-schoolers and their parents, but any collector would savor every word and picture on each and every one of the 32-40 pages. A subscription was reasonably priced at $7 per year. The high cost of producing the high quality, full color magazine proved to be prohibitive. The Snoopy Magazine was published much too briefly.

Snoopy Magazine. Fall, 1988. $10-15

Snoopy Magazine, Premier Issue. Winter, 1988.
$12-20

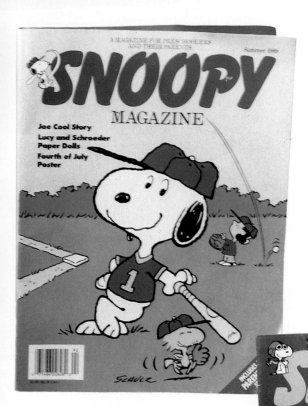

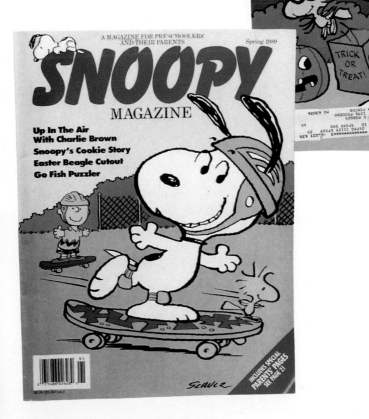

Snoopy Magazine. Summer, 1989. $10-15

Snoopy Magazine. Spring, 1990. $10-15

Snoopy Magazine. Fall, 1989. $10-15

Snoopy Magazine. Spring, 1989. $10-15

Snoopy Magazine. Winter, 1990. $10-15

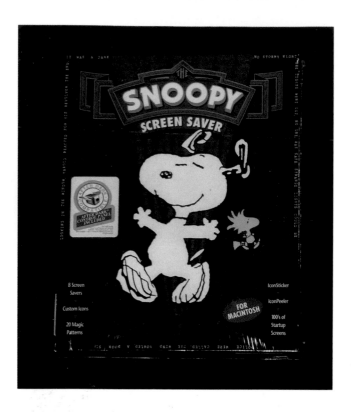

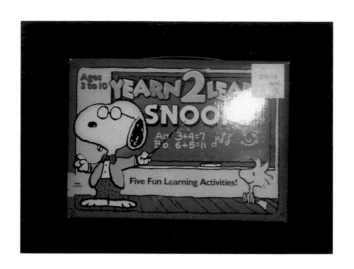

"Yearn 2 Learn" game pack software. Image Smith Inc. 1990s. $30-40

"Snoopy Screen Saver" for computer. 1990s. $15-20

"Yearn 2 Learn." Contains five activity software programs. Image Smith Inc. 1990s. $30-40

"Yearn 2 Learn" activity software. Image Smith Inc. 1990s. $15-20 each

Snoopy "Yearn 2 Learn" and "Snoopy's Game Club" computer software. Left: Image Smith Inc. 1990s. $45-50; right: Accolade, 1990s. $15-20 each

SNOOPY'S WARDROBE AND ACCESSORIES

WHAT TO WEAR?

Denim Snoopy child's vest. 1980s. $5-8

Knit sweater with Snoopy skating in the snow. Design on front only. Bill Ditford. 1992. No longer made. $125-150

Cotton sailor shirt. J.G. Hook. Late 1980s-early 1990s. $25-35

Knit Snoopy tennis sweater. 1980s. $60-70

Knit sweater with Snoopy as Christopher Columbus, commemorating the 500th anniversary of the discovery of America. Design on front and back. Bill Ditford design. 1992. No longer made. $185-225

Knit sweater with Snoopy giving flowers to Woodstock. "Snoopy and Friends." Mid-1990s. $25-35

Knit sweater, "Ski Bum." Devo Inc. 1980s. $60-70

Snoopy adult's Arrow sweater, acrylic. Early 1980s. $40-50

Cotton, sequinned Snoopy sailor shirt. Marisa. Early 1990s. $90-120

Cotton Snoopy sweat shirt. French slogan reads "I'm allergic to morning." 1980s. $25-30

Genus blue jean jacket. 1995-96. Genus lost its license for Peanuts products in 1996. $200-250

I'M VERY COLD!

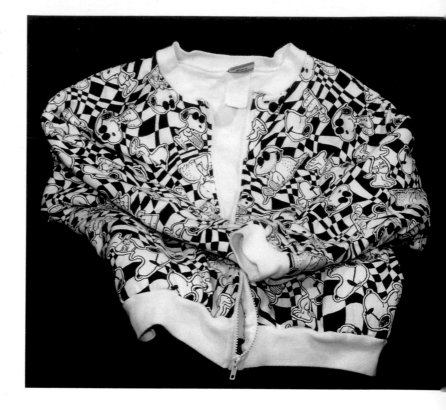

Quilted jacket. 1990s. $30-40. Featured at Camp Snoopy, Knotts Berry farm.

Box of "Snoopy Slipper Socks." 1990s. $5-7

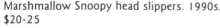

Plush Snoopy earmuffs. 1980s/90s. $10-15

Plush Snoopy children's slippers. 1990s.
$10-12

Marshmallow Snoopy head slippers. 1990s.
$20-25

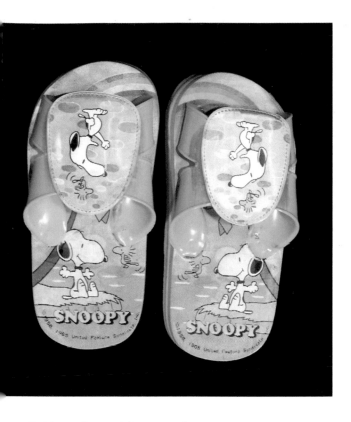

Rubber swim sandals. 1980s. $4-6

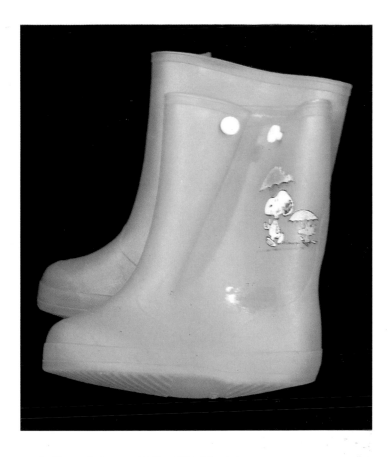

Rubber rain boots. 1980s. $12-15 mint

Rubber "Snoopers" rain boots. 1980s. $12-15 mint

Rubber red rain boots. 1980s. $12-15 mint

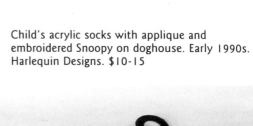

Child's acrylic socks with applique and embroidered Snoopy on doghouse. Early 1990s. Harlequin Designs. $10-15

Knit hat and knit socks, gift boxed. Accessory Network. Mid-1990s. $10-15

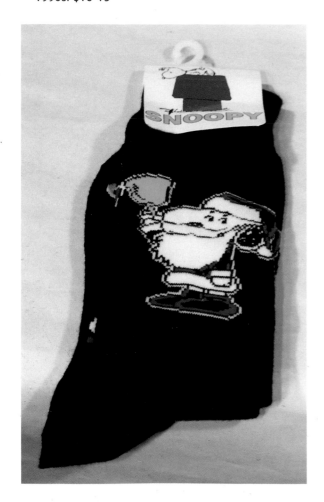

Men's acrylic Santa Snoopy socks. 1990s. High Point Knitting Inc. $7-10

Men's acrylic Snoopy Halloween socks. 1990s. High Point Knitting Inc. $7-10

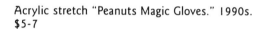

Acrylic stretch "Peanuts Magic Gloves." 1990s.
$5-7

Acrylic Snoopy socks. Through the 1990s High Point Knitting Inc. made many patterns of wonderful socks for children, women and men. $4-6.

Ties. Black and white polyester tie by Cervantes, 1980s. $20-25. Maroon silk tie, 1990s. $20-30

Silk and knit Snoopy golf ties. Mid-1990s. Silk $20-25-Knit $10-15

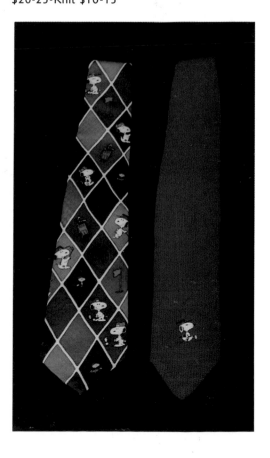

"Snoopy Mitten Clips" from Butterfly. 1980s.
$5-7

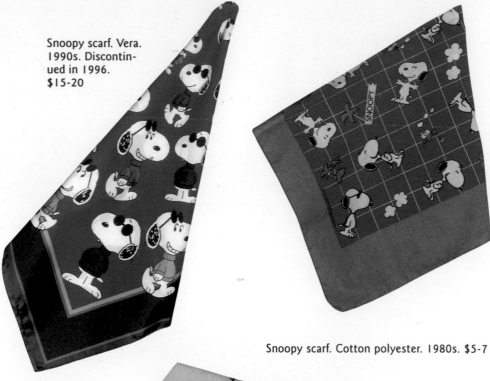

Snoopy scarf. Vera. 1990s. Discontinued in 1996. $15-20

Snoopy scarf. Cotton polyester. 1980s. $5-7

Snoopy and Woodstock scarf. Vera. 1990s. Discontinued in 1996. $15-20

Scout Snoopy cotton polyester neck scarf. 1980s. $5-7

Cotton Snoopy and Woodstock, child's handkerchief from Japan. Hallmark. 1990s. $12-18

Cotton Snoopy child's handkerchief from Japan. Hallmark. 1990s. $12-18

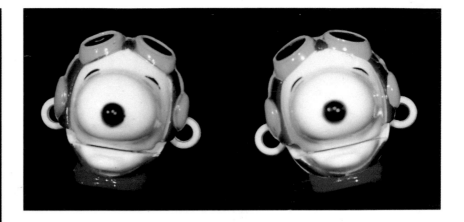

Flying Ace, plastic head, "Bow Biters." Brooksides. 1980. $3-5

"Team Snoopy Wet Suit." 1990s. $25-30

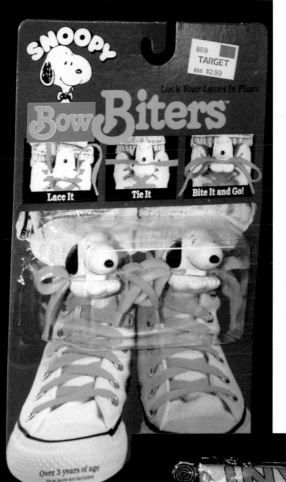

"Bow Biters" by Brookside
Plastic Corp. 1990s. $4-6
Also came as Flying Ace.

Cotton adult tee shirt.
"Rainy Days in London".
Blues. 1980s. $20-25

Shoe lace decorations. Flying Ace. Brooksides.
1990s. $4-6

BELTS

Elastic Snoopy child's belt. 1980s. $4-6

Gift boxed wallet and key chain and scarf set. Accessory Network. Mid-1990s. $10-15.

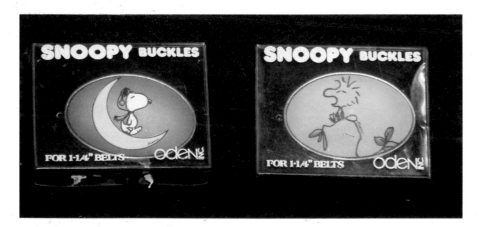

Snoopy belt buckles from Adens, Inc. Embossed leather with metal base. 1980s. $15-20

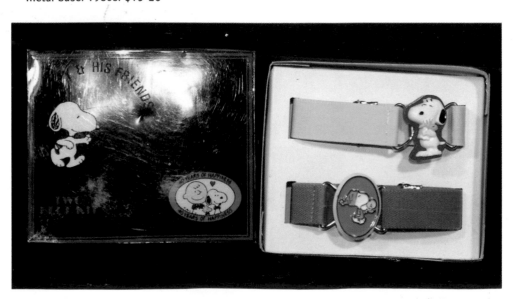

Elastic Snoopy child's suspenders. Lee Co. 1980s. $10-12

Elastic children's belts with plastic buckles. 1980s. $10-12 set with box

COME SEW WITH ME

"Snoopy Patch L.A. 84" fabric Olympic patches. Determined Productions. $7-10 each

Snoopy and Peanuts patterns from Simplicity. 1980s. $12-18

"Snoopy" and "Belle" "Patch L.A. 84" fabric Olympic patches. Determined. $7-10 each

Plastic buttons from JHB International. Early 1990s. $3-5 each package

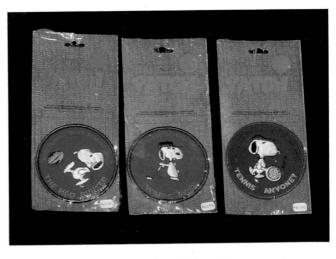

"Snoopy Patch L.A. 84" washable/iron on/sew on fabric patches. Commemorating the 1984 Olympics in Los Angeles. 12 varieties available. Determined. $7-10 each

Fabric Snoopy sports patches. Early 1970s. Determined. Matches pillows stuffed with Kapok. 3". $6-8 each

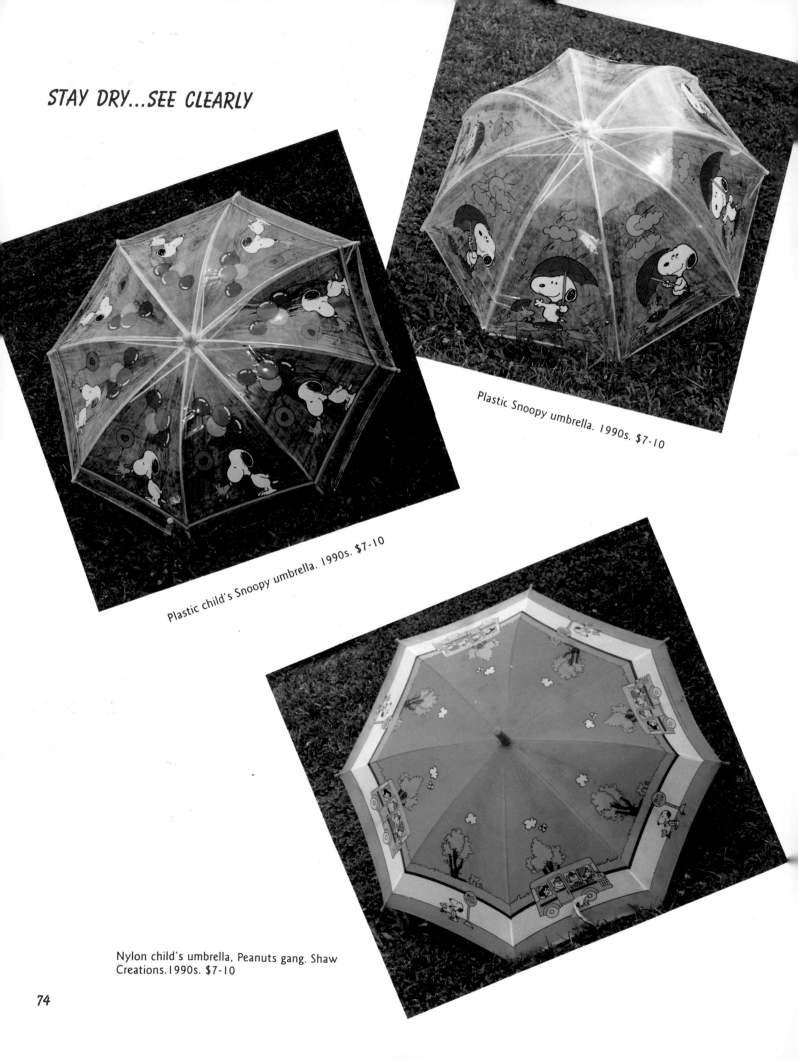

STAY DRY...SEE CLEARLY

Plastic Snoopy umbrella. 1990s. $7-10

Plastic child's Snoopy umbrella. 1990s. $7-10

Nylon child's umbrella, Peanuts gang. Shaw
Creations.1990s. $7-10

Snoopy and Joe Cool plastic sun glasses. Right: Mid-1990s. Metal $7-10. Left· 1980s-1990s. Plastic. $3-4

Vinyl eye glass case on chain. Snoopy on front. $15-20

Vinyl eye glass cases. $15-20 each

Vinyl eye glass cases. $15-20 each

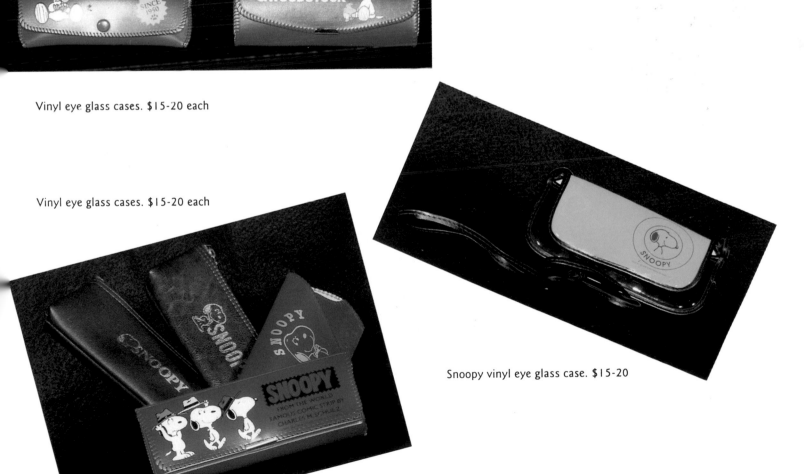

Snoopy vinyl eye glass case. $15-20

SNOOPY TO GO: PURSES, TOTES, AND TRAVEL BAGS

Snoopy coin purses. Various makers including Hallmark. 1980s.
$6-8 each

Snoopy wallets. Variety of makers including
Quantasia and Butterfly. 1980s-90s. $8-15 each

Vinyl wallets. Early 1980s. $12-15 each

Canvas mini
Snoopy bag. 1980s.
$3-5

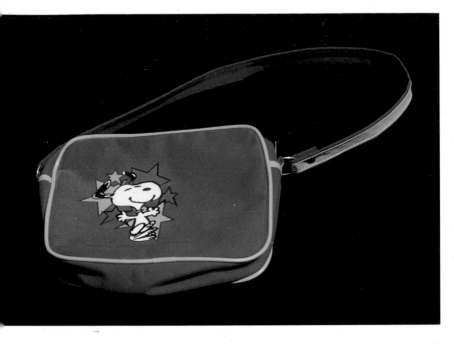

Canvas Snoopy purse. 1970s. $12-15

Fabric carry-all bag. 1980s. $10-15

Canvas Snoopy "Love" tote bag. 1970s. $12-15

Canvas Snoopy tote bag. Determined. 1980s. $10-12

Fabric Christmas Snoopy purse. Horizon Designs. Mid-1990s. $10-12

Vinyl tote bag. "Snoopy's Astro Bag." Natco Products Corp. 1969. $25-35

Fabric carry-all bag. Butterfly. Late 1970s-1980s. $7-10

Fabric carry all bag. 1990s. $10-15

Fabric Snoopy tote bag. Cut and sew fabric. 1970s. $8-12

Plastic see-thru carry-all bag. Sanrio. Japan. 1990s. $8-12

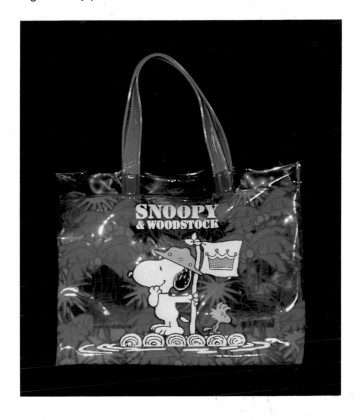

Plastic Scout Snoopy and Woodstock bag. Phoenix Corp. Ltd. Japan. 1990s. $8-12

Plastic see-thru carry-all bag. Phoenix Corp. Ltd. Japan. 1990s. $8-12

Plastic Snoopy tote bags. Sanrio, 1990s. Japan. $8-10 each

Fabric Snoopy sports bag. 1980s. $15-20

Fabric carry-all bag. Horizon Kids. Early 1990s. $12-20

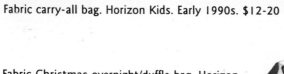

Fabric Christmas overnight/duffle bag. Horizon Designs. Mid-1990s. $15-20

Vinyl Snoopy head purse. Jaclyn Inc. 1996. $15-20

Fabric Christmas Snoopy purse. Horizon Designs. Mid-1990s. $10-12

Fabric back pack. Accessory Network. 1990s.
$15-20

Plastic Snoopy and
Woodstock duffle bag.
Accessory Network. 1990s.
$15-20

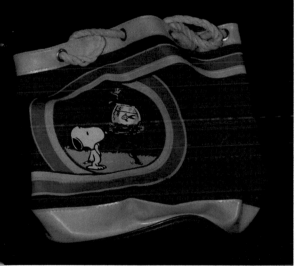

Fabric swim bag. Butterfly. 1980s. $15-20 mint

Fabric beach bag. Butterfly.
1980s. $15-20

Fabric beach bag. Butterfly. 1980s. $15-20

Fabric beach bag.
Horizon Kids.
1990s. $15-20

Nylon "Jets" sports bag.
Quantasia. 1980s. $15-20

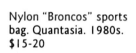

Nylon "Giants" sports bag.
Quantasia. 1980s. $15-20

Nylon "Broncos" sports
bag. Quantasia. 1980s.
$15-20

Nylon "Chiefs" sports bag.
Quantasia. 1980s. $15-20
Quantasia made a variety
of products with different
teams including wallets,
large duffles, roll bags, and
more.

Canvas suitcase. Armored Luggage Mfg. Co.
1970s. $25-35

Canvas suitcase. Aviva. 1980s. $30-40

Vinyl suitcase. Quantasia.
1980s. $40-50

Fabric suitcase from Aviva. Flying Ace. Early
1980s. $30-40

Vinyl Snoopy suitcase. 1990s. Came in two sizes. $40-60

SNOOPY'S HOLIDAY

VALENTINE'S DAY

Cotton Snoopys. Applause valentine selection. 1990s. $6-8 each

Cardboard valentine centerpiece from Hallmark. 1980s. $15-20
mint

Snoopy snack canisters. Sold with cheese or caramel popcorn.
1980s. $7-9 each

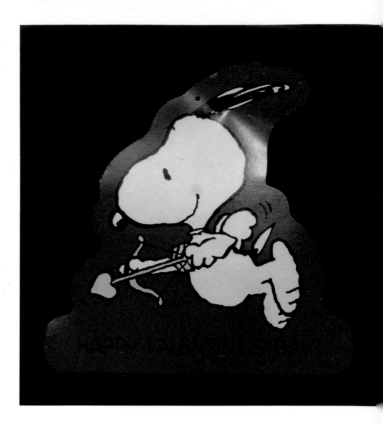

Valentine's day greeting card. Hallmark. 1990s. $2-3

"Snoopy Valentines" in
doghouse box, from
Hallmark. 1970s. $20-25

Dancing Snoopy and Woodstock booklet.
1990s. Japan. $4-6

"Peanuts Valentines" in doghouse box, from
Hallmark. 1970s. $20-25

Packages of valentines from Hallmark. 1990s. $3-5

TO MY SWEETHEART

I WANTED TO GET YOU SOMETHING EXTRA SPECIAL FOR VALENTINE'S DAY!

Sweetheart greeting card. Hallmark. 1980s. $4-5

"Snoopy and Woodstock" valentines. Ambassador. 1990s. $3-5

Ceramic love coffee cups. $8-15 each

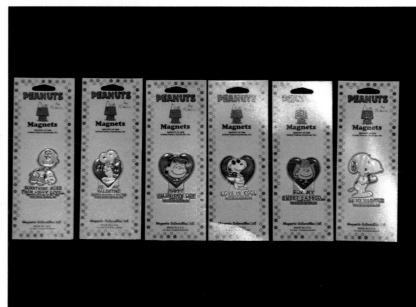

Variety of Valentine refrigerator magnets. Mid-1990s. Magnetic Collectibles Inc. $3-4 each

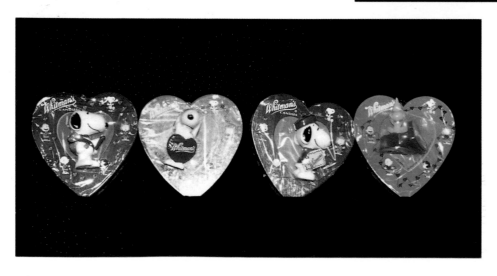

Valentine candy with Snoopy or Woodstock fun figure on front from Whitman's. Mid-1990s. $3-4

ST. PAT'S DAY

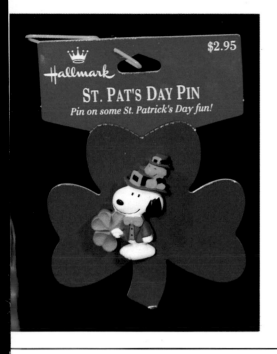

Cotton St. Patrick's Day Snoopy rag dolls. 4.5". Applause. 1991.
$6-8 each

Plastic St. Patrick's Day pin from Hallmark. 1996. $3-4

THE EASTER BEAGLE IS COMING!

Easter "Peanuts Press-out Decorations" from Hallmark. 1970s.
$15-20 mint

Cardboard Easter basket. Hallmark. Early 1980s. $5-7

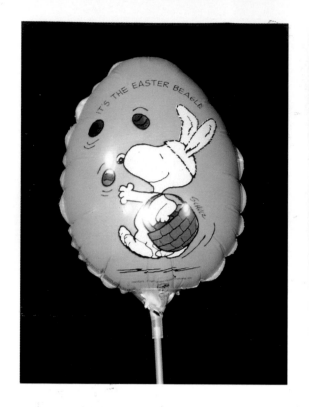

Resin Easter "Keepsake Ornaments." Hallmark. 1995-1996. $12-15

Mylar balloon on a stick. 1980s/90s. $2-3

Ceramic "Springtime Mini Figurines." Snoopy in different poses. Willitts. 1990. $30-35 set

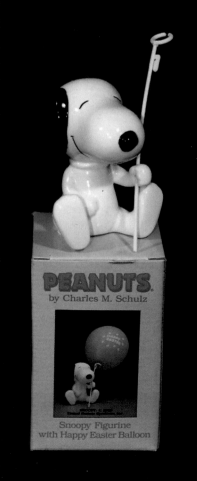

Snoopy figurine with "Happy Easter" balloon from Willitts. 1990. $15-20

Hallmark Easter Snoopy pin. Hallmark. 1995.
$3-4

Plush Easter Beagle. Determined. Late 1980s.
$15-20

Ceramic Easter egg ornament. Napkin ring base
not included. Willitts. 1990. $10-15

Tricot Easter Beagles. Came in small Whitman's Easter baskets.
1995. $4-6

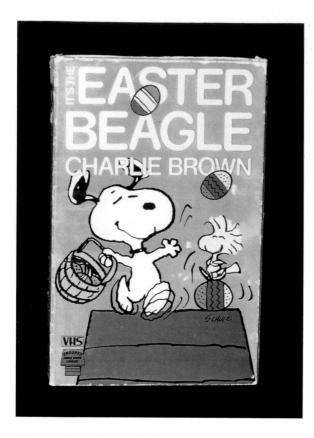

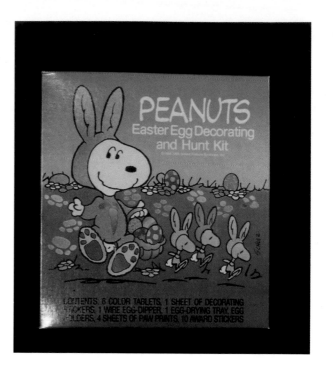

Easter egg decorating kit. Hallmark. Early 1990s. $4-6

"It's the Easter Beagle Charlie Brown" VHS video. 1974. $10-12

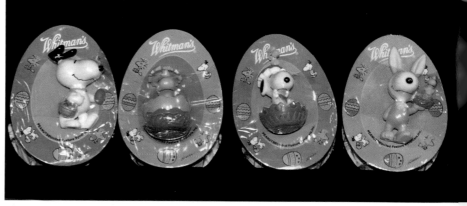

Easter egg with bubble gum inside. Leaf Co. Mid-1990s. $2-3

Easter candy with Snoopy or Woodstock fun figure on front from Whitman's. Mid-1990s. $3-4

Plastic Easter egg banks filled with candy from Whitman's. 1996. $6-10

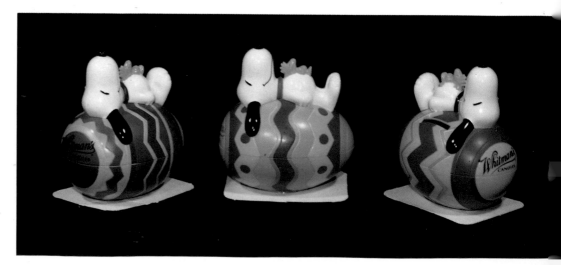

Small Easter basket from Whitman's Chocolate Co. Mid-1990s. $8-10

Large Easter basket from Whitman's Chocolate Co. Mid-1990s. $15-20

Snoopy as Easter Beagle, egg wraps. (Place egg, in wrap, into boiling water. It then shrinks to fit egg perfectly.) Hallmark. 1980s. $7-10 per dozen

"Snoopy and Peanuts Gang Egg Decorating Kit." Easter Unlimited. Late 1980s. $4-6

HALLOWEEN

Paper plates, cups, napkins, table cover. Halloween collection. Hallmark. 1990s. $4-11

Plastic Halloween decoration. Flashing light. Hallmark. Early 1990s. $7-10

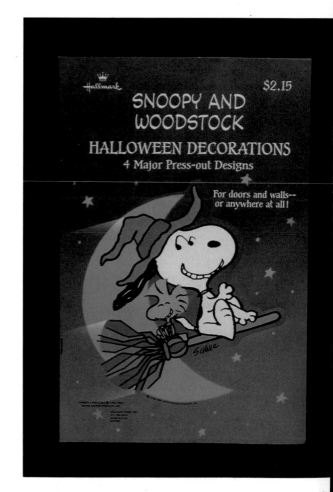

Snoopy Halloween invitations from Hallmark. Early 1990s. $4-5

"Snoopy and Woodstock Halloween Decorations" from Hallmark. Early 1990s. $4-5

"Snoopy Pumpkin Cutter." Early 1990s. $5-8

Dracula Snoopy Halloween decoration. Hallmark. 1980s. $3-4

Halloween Snoopy fun figures with boxed candy from Whitman's. 1995. $2-3

Halloween decoration, Snoopy in mask and cape. Hallmark. 1990s. $2-3

Plastic Halloween mask. Accompanied inexpensive vinyl children's costume. 1980s-90s. $4-6 mask alone.

Halloween candy from Whitman's. Mid-1990s. $1-2

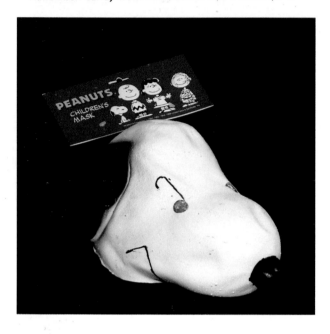

Rubber Snoopy children's mask. Topstone Industries. 1994. $10-15

Plastic Snoopy Halloween costume with mask. Collegeville Costumes. 1980s. $15-20 in box.

Plastic Flying Ace adult mask. 1990s. $60-75

TURKEY TIME

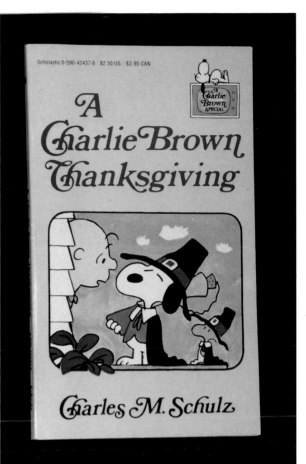

A Charlie Brown Thanksgiving story book. Paperback. Scholastic. 1970s. $4-6

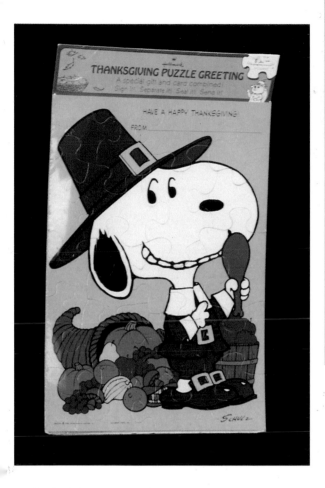

Thanksgiving puzzle and greeting card. Hallmark. 1980s. $8-12

Thanksgiving card. with Snoopy as a pilgrim. Hallmark. 1980s. 12" $3-4. 3 feet. $10-15.

Thanksgiving decoration with Snoopy eating turkey leg. Hallmark. 1980s. $3-4

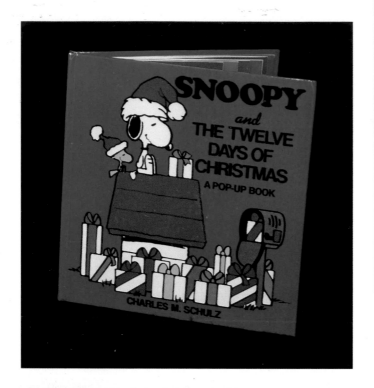

Willitts Christmas votive candle holder. Late 1980s. $20-30

Snoopy and the Twelve Days of Christmas, pop up book. Inside view. 1980s. $20-25

Crocheted Snoopy ornament. Determined. 1980s. $15-20

Silver-tone Christmas ornament. Determined.
1980s. $12-18

Gold-tone Christmas ornament. Determined.
1980s. $12-18

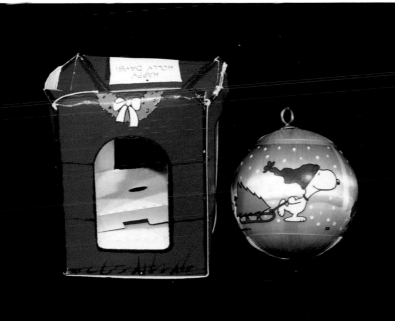

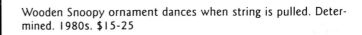

Wooden Snoopy ornament dances when string is pulled. Determined. 1980s. $15-25

Snoopy satin Christmas ornament. Doghouse-shaped box.
Hallmark. 1978. $18-22

Ceramic Snoopy with Christmas tree by
Determined Productions. 2.75". 1975. $15-20

"Snoopy and friends Satin Christmas Ornament." Determined
Productions. 1980s. $15-20

Ceramic Snoopy on present ornament.
Determined Productions. 1970s. $8-12

Ceramic English Snoopy, ornament, Determined 3". 1977. $20-30.
Other in the International Series but not pictured: Mexico, Snoopy
in sombrero; Germany, Tyrolene outfit; Spain, bullfighting outfit;
England, palace guard outfit; Scandanavia, with viking helmet;
Japan, wearing kimono; Transylvania, cape and top hat. $20-30
each.

Ceramic Snoopy with candy cane by Determined Productions. 2.25". 1975. $10-15

Ceramic Snoopy playing cello by Determined Prod. 1976. 2.5". $20-25 Other in the Musician Series, but not pictured: Peppermint Patty playing guitar; Linus playing tenor sax; Charlie Brown playing bass drum; and Lucy playing trumpet. $20-30 each.

Flat ceramic ornament from Determined Productions, 1978. 3". $20-30. Others in set but not shown are: Woodstock on package; Snoopy leaping with candy cane; Snoopy carrying Woodstock atop a package; and Snoopy wearing red and green stripped stocking hat. In another set not pictured from Determined Productions, 1980 are: Snoopy lying on wreath; Woodstock on Noel; Snoopy carrying Christmas tree; Snoopy angel; Santa Snoopy going down chimney; and Woodstock angel. $20-30 each

Ceramic Snoopy holding wreath, ornament by Determined Productions. 1975. $15-20

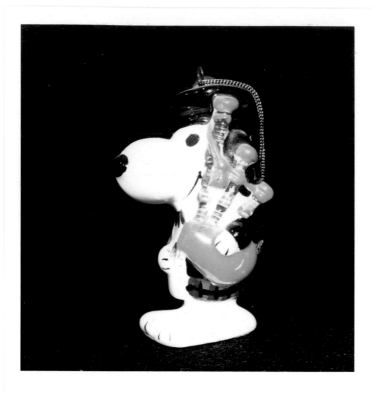

Ceramic Snoopy Scottish bagpipe player, ornament. International Series. Determined Productions, 1977. $20-25

Ceramic India Snoopy ornament, by Determined Productions. International Series. 3". 1977. $20-25

Ceramic Italian Snoopy from International Series by Determined. 1977. $20-25

Ceramic French Snoopy artist from International Series by Determined. 1977. $20-25

Plastic Snoopy in blue race car ornament. 1980s. $3-5.

Ceramic Snoopy Santa in car ornament. Vehicle Series by Determined Products. 2.5". 1979. $20-25

Ceramic Snoopy in boat with tree, ornament. Vehicle Series. 2.5". 1979. $20-25. Others from the Vehicle Series but not shown: Santa Woodstock in firetruck and Santa Snoopy in steam engine. $20-25 each

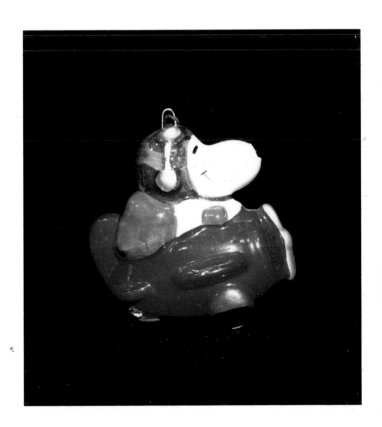

Ceramic Flying Ace Snoopy ornament, from Vehicle Series by Determined Productions. 1979. $20-25

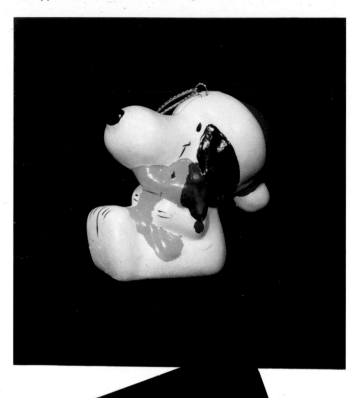

Ceramic Snoopy detective ornament from Adventure Series. By Determined Products. 1975. 2.75". Others in the series but not shown: Clown, Robin hood, Davy Crockett, Indian, Bandit. $20-25 each.

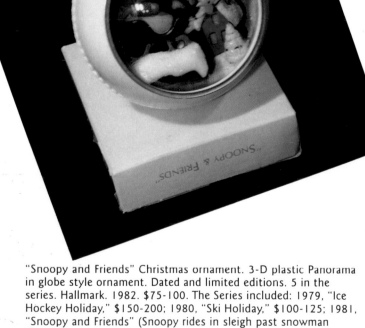

"Snoopy and Friends" Christmas ornament. 3-D plastic Panorama in globe style ornament. Dated and limited editions. 5 in the series. Hallmark. 1982. $75-100. The Series included: 1979, "Ice Hockey Holiday," $150-200; 1980, "Ski Holiday," $100-125; 1981, "Snoopy and Friends" (Snoopy rides in sleigh past snowman shaped like Snoopy), $75-100; 1982, "Snoopy and Friends" as shown; 1983, "Santa Snoopy," $60-90

Willitts miniature snowball Snoopy ornament. Early 1990s. $15-20

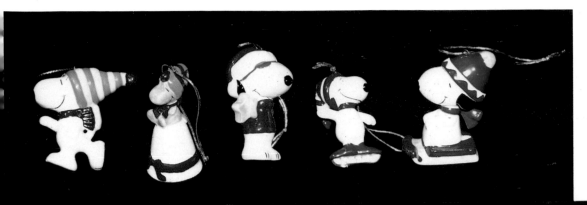

Willitts various ceramic Christmas ornaments. 1980s-90s. $15-25 each

Porcelain ornament, Snoopy riding carousel horse. Willitts. Late 1980s. $25-35

Porcelain disc ornament from Willitts. Snoopy on doghouse, 1990. $15-20

Porcelain disc ornament with Snoopy, Charlie Brown, and Woodstock from Willitts. 1990. $15-20

Ceramic micro mini bells. 1" x 1". "Genuine bone china, Taiwan". Early 1980s. $15-20. Not pictured: Snoopy lying on dog house; Charlie Brown eating candy cane; Snoopy opening gifts; Santa Snoopy giving Lucy gift; Snoopy holds Woodstock with decorated nest. $15-20 each.

Ceramic Christmas bell ornament. 1980s. $20-30

Ceramic Christmas bell. 1977. Schmid. $30-40

Willitts porcelain Christmas ornament. 1989. $15-25 in box

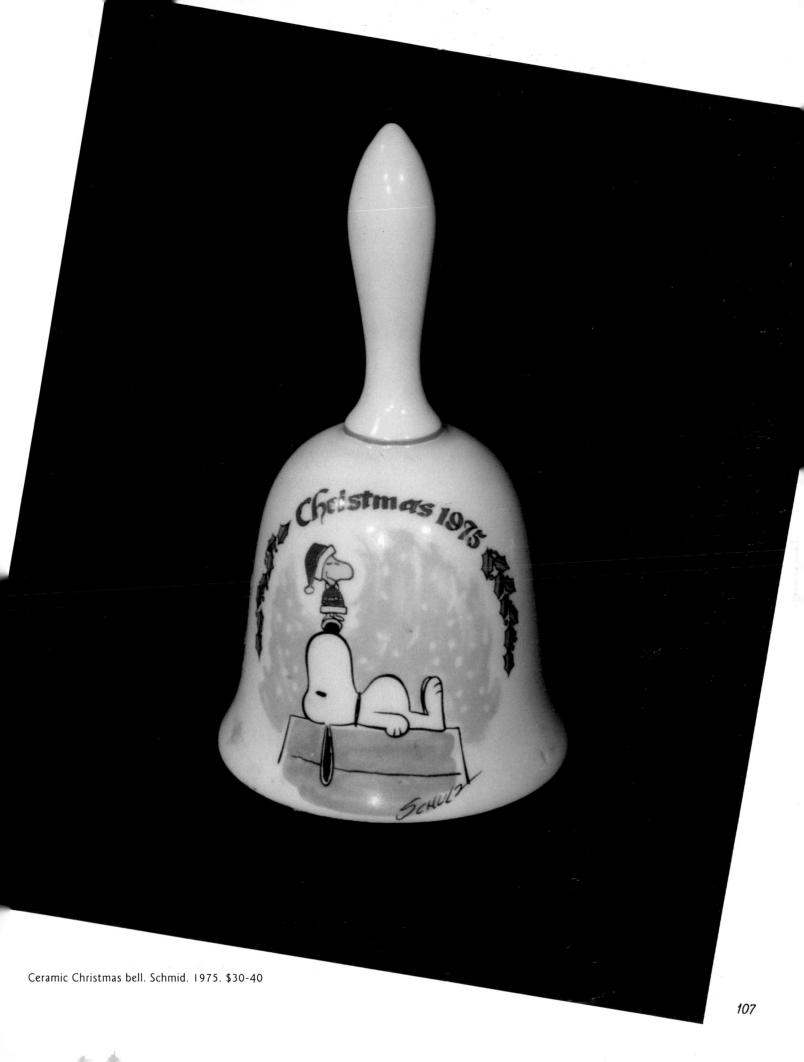

Ceramic Christmas bell. Schmid. 1975. $30-40

Plastic "Stocking Hanger." Hallmark. Early 1980s. $30-40

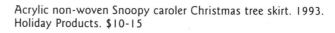

Snoopy with gift and Woodstock sitting on gift mini candles. Hallmark, 1990s.. $5-8 each

Acrylic non-woven Snoopy caroler Christmas tree skirt. 1993. Holiday Products. $10-15

Styrafoam Christmas ornament. 1980s. $10-15

Fleece Santa
Snoopy Christmas
stocking. 1980s.
$15-20

Cotton Snoopy Christmas stocking. Determined. 1980s. $15-20

Acrylic knit Snoopy
Christmas stocking.
1980s. $15-20

Cotton Snoopy
Christmas stocking.
1980s. $15-20

Acrylic non-woven
Christmas stockings.
Holiday Products. 16".
1993. $4-6

Acrylic non-woven Christmas stocking.
Holiday Products. 16". 1993. $4-6 each

Acrylic non-woven mini Christmas stockings.
Holiday Products. 1993. $4-6 set

"Holiday Card Assortment" from Hallmark. 1990s. $8-12

Party Christmas coasters from Hallmark. 1980s. $7-10

Box of Snoopy Christmas cards. Hallmark. Mid-1990s. $15-20

Package of "Christmas Cards for Kids." Hallmark. 1990s. $4-6

Paper, Christmas placemat from Hallmark. 1970s. $3-5 each

Cardboard Christmas puzzle. Hallmark. 1980s. $8-12

Holiday greeting puzzle from Hallmark. 1980s. $8-12

Advent calendar from Hallmark. 1990s. $5-7

Christmas greeting card and door decoration.
Hallmark. 1990s. $4-5

Inflatable Christmas Snoopy Santa for outdoors. Intex. Late
1980s. $15-20

Tin Snoopy Christmas tray. Willitts. 1990. $15-20

Cotton Christmas pot holders. 1990s. Cannon.
$4-7 each

Terry cloth Christmas towels. Cannon. 1990s.
$5-8

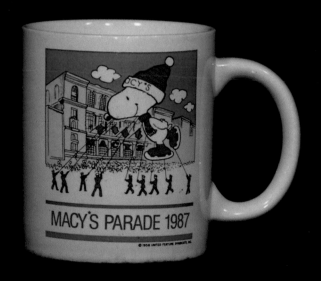

Ceramic Macy's Parade 1987 coffee cup. $8-14
each

Holiday towel and oven mit set. Barth and
Dreyfuss. 1990s. $10-15 set

Ceramic Christmas coffee cups. Willitts. 1990s. $7-12 each

Ceramic Christmas coffee cups. Determined. 1980s. $8-15 each

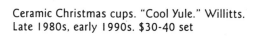

Ceramic Christmas cups. "Cool Yule." Willitts. Late 1980s, early 1990s. $30-40 set

Cotton Snoopy Christmas carry-all. Horizon Kids. 1994. $15-20

Cotton Christmas apron with cookie cutters.
Horizon Designs. Mid-1990s. $15-20

Fabric Christmas purses. Horizon Kids. 1994.
$12-15 each

Plastic holiday waste basket. Saturday Knight
Ltd. 1990s. $20-25

"3-Piece Bath Set." Saturday Knight Ltd. 1990s $10-15

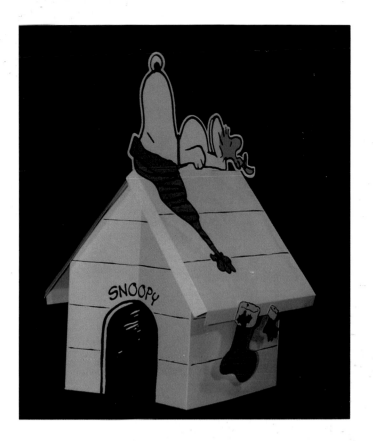

Christmas Snoopy cardboard display. 1990s. $10-15

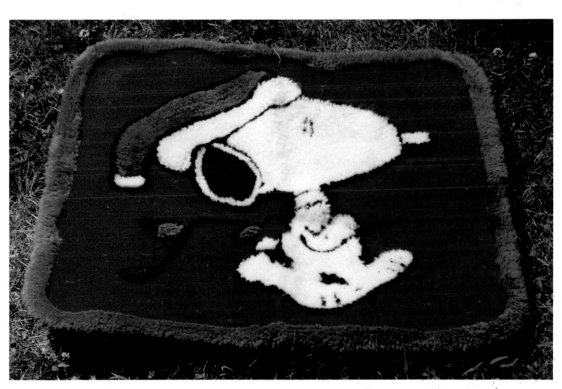

Christmas Snoopy throw rug. Saturday Knight Ltd. Early 1990s. $20-25

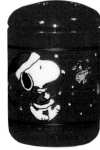

Christmas plastic bathroom set. Saturday Knight Ltd. 1990s. $15-20

Christmas welcome mat, indoor or outdoor. Bacova Guild Ltd. Olefin Carpets. 1990s. $10-15

Christmas Snoopy ornaments with boxed candy from Whitman's. 1995. $4-5

Christmas door mat. "And a beagle in a pear tree." Bacova Guild Ltd. Olefin carpets. 1990s. $10-15

"Kids Zipper Pull" from Hallmark. 1995. $4-6

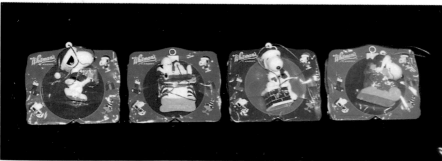

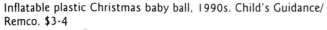

Christmas ornaments on box of Whitman's Chocolates. 1995. $4-5

Inflatable plastic Christmas baby ball, 1990s. Child's Guidance/Remco. $3-4

PARTY TIME

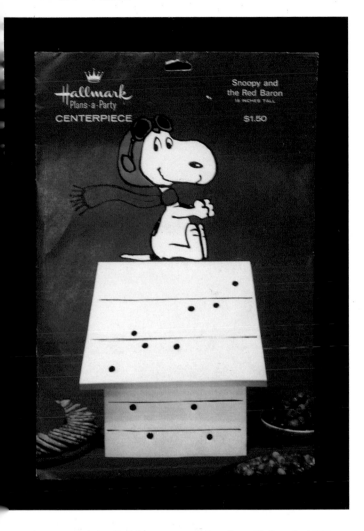

"Party Door Decoration" from Hallmark. 1990s. $5-7

Cardboard Snoopy tiny gift box. Hallmark.
1980s-90s. $2-3

Snoopy and the Red Baron centerpiece from Hallmark. 1970s.
$20-25

Plastic "Snoopy Party Picks" from Hallmark.
1970s. $8-12

SNOOPY'S SPORTS WORLD

LET'S GO SWIMMING

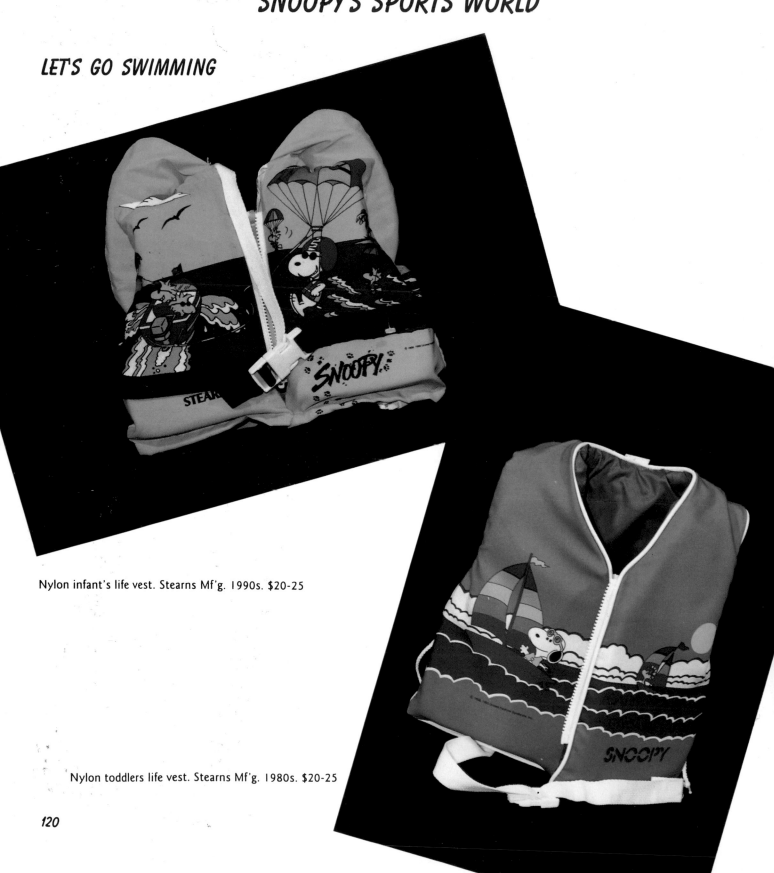

Nylon infant's life vest. Stearns Mf'g. 1990s. $20-25

Nylon toddlers life vest. Stearns Mf'g. 1980s. $20-25

Nylon youth life vest. 1980s. $20-25

Plastic Snoopy fishing bobber. Zebco. 1980s/
1990s. $3-5

Nylon "Snoopy Catch 'em" tote. Zebco. Holds tackle, bait, worms, hooks. 1990s. $4-7.

Snoopy fishing pole. Zebco. 1980s/90s. $10-15

Plastic inflatable beach ball. 1990s. Japan. $4-6

Inflatable swim vest. "The Wet Set." Intex. 1990s. $6-9

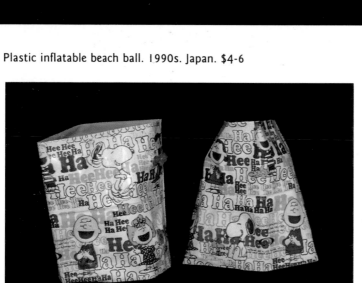

Vinyl water wings. Mattel. $5-8.

Vinyl pool toys. "The Wet Set." Intex. 1990s.
Boat: $15-20. Toys: $4-6

Plastic inflatable air mats. "The Wet Set."
Intex. 1990s. $15-20

Mylar Snoopy kite. 1980s. Crinden Martin Mf'g. $8-12

Mylar Snoopy kite. Crinden Martin Mf'g. 1980s. $8-11

Plastic Snoopy kites. 1980s. Right: $6-8. Left: Met Life-free promotion. Early 1990s. $3-4

Plastic Flying Ace kite. Late 1970s. $6-10

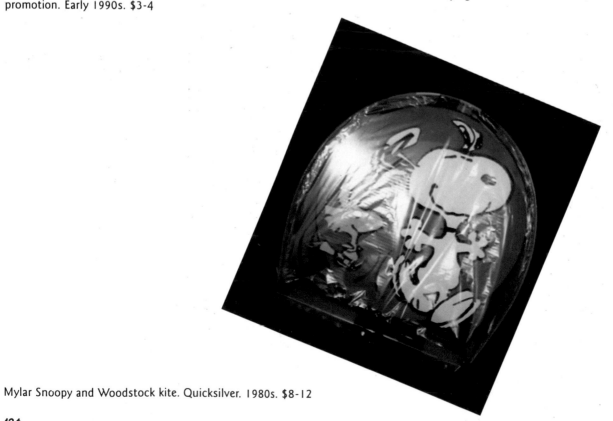

Mylar Snoopy and Woodstock kite. Quicksilver. 1980s. $8-12

PLAY BALL!

Wilson Charlie Brown football. 1969. $150-175

Linus mini poster. Hallmark.
1980s. $3-5

Leather "Fotoball" football. 1995. $20-25

Leather Snoopy "Fotoball" baseball and glove. 1995. $20-25

Plastic Peanuts baseball. Part of Playskool "Snoopy Slugger" included with oversized yellow bat and orange/white cap. Late 1970s. Ball $5-7 as is. $30-40 set

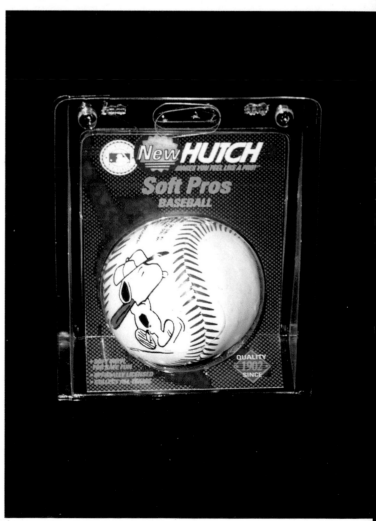

Leather Charlie Brown "Fotoball" baseball and glove. 1995. $20-25

Snoopy baseball. Hutch-soft vinyl. 1990s. $10-15

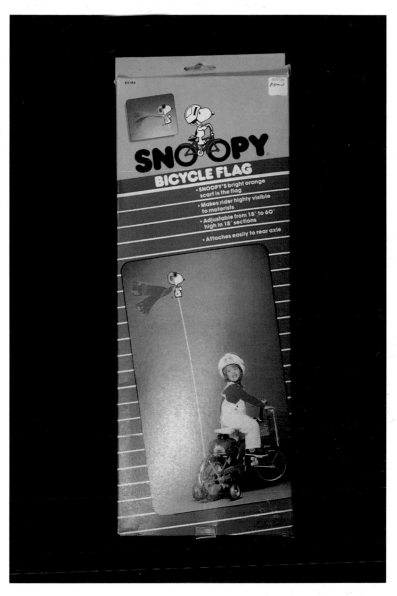

Bicycle flag with Flying Ace on end. AC International. 1980s & 1990s. $15-20

Plastic water bottle. AC International. 1980s-1990s $5-7

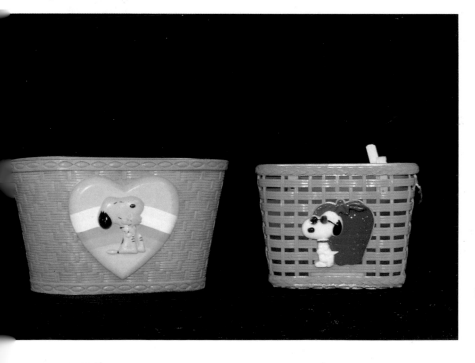

Plastic bicycle baskets. 1980s-90s. $5-8

Handlebar toy and bicycle horn. AC International. 1980s-90s.
$4-7

Plastic bike siren. AC International. 1980s
& 1990s. $12-16

Bicycle spoke reflectors. Snoopy on bike.
Hallmark. 1980s. $8-10

Metal bicycle bells. AC International. 1980s-90s. $4-7

Metal Peanuts license plate from Hallmark. 1980s. $8-10

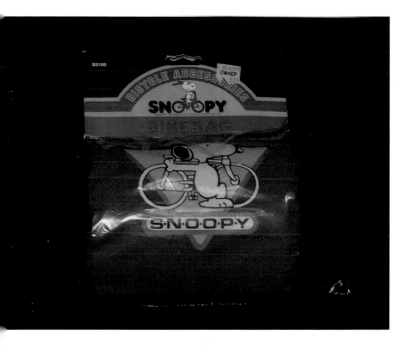

Plastic "Snoopy Bike Bag." Butterfly/Hollywood Accessories. 1980s. $8-12

Nylon back pack. Butterfly/Hollywood Accessories. 1980s. $15-20

SNOOPY'S MUSIC

Wooden music box. Flying Ace from Anri. 1969. $80-100.

Wooden music box. Snoopy with doghouse from Anri. 1971. $125-150

Wooden Flying Ace music box. Schmid. 1971. $100-150

Wooden music box. Snoopy on doghouse as astronaut. Schmid, 1971 $75-100

Wooden Flying Ace music box. Schmid,1973. $100-175

Musical ceramic mug, Flying Ace. Schmid. Early 1970s. $50-60

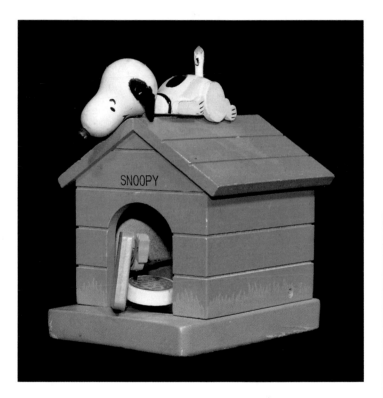

Wooden Snoopy on doghouse, music box. Woodstock carries coin inside. Schmid, 1971. $90-110

Wooden music box with drawer by Aviva. Ceramic Snoopy revolves with music. 1974. $60 90

Ceramic Snoopy skiing, music box by Aviva.
1973. $40-55

Fabric Quantasia music box. 1980s. $45-60
Others not shown: Belle in arobic pose; Snoopy
on drum; Snoopy holding ball; Snoopy atop
black hat; Baby Snoopy with bib and bottle.
$45-60 each

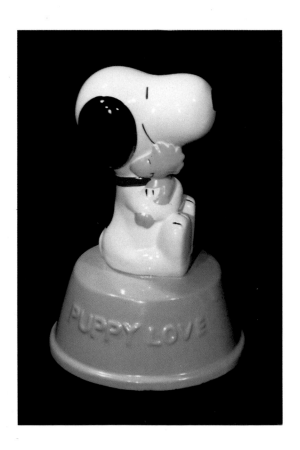

Plastic "Snoopy & Woodstock" music box.
Quantasia. Mid-1980s. $30-40

Ceramic Snoopy music box. Willitts. 1990.
$40-60

Ceramic Snoopy music box. Aviva. Mid-1970s. $40-55

Ceramic Snoopy atop dog house music box by Aviva. 1974. $30-40

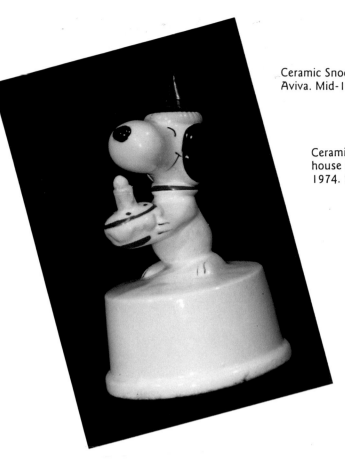

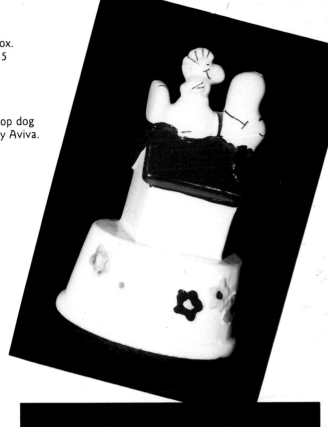

Ceramic Flying Ace music box. Willitts. 1989. $40-60

Ceramic Snoopy caroler music box by Willitts. 1988. $45-65

Ceramic Soccer player music box made by Willitts. 1989. $40-60

Ceramic Easter Beagle music box made by Willitts. 1990. $40-60

Ceramic Christmas house music box made by Willitts. 1989. $40-60

Ceramic Santa Snoopy music box by Willitts. 1990. $40-60

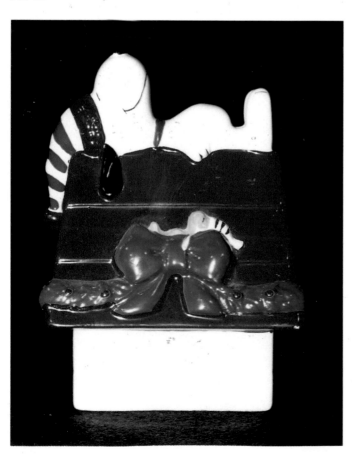

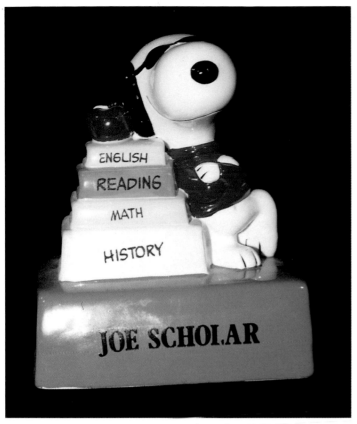

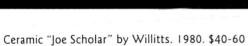

Ceramic "Joe Scholar" by Willitts. 1980. $40-60

Snoopy on musical carousel horse. Willitts. 1989. $100-125

Resin Snoopy and Woodstock music box. Willitts. Beaglefest
commemorative, very few made. 1993. $65-85

Snoopy on doghouse Christmas glitter dome. Willitts. 1990. $50-60

Snoopy in sleigh, revolving snow dome. Willitts. 1989. $40-50

Snoopy conductor in dome. Revolving band. Willitts. 1991. $50-60

Christmas revolving Snoopy snow dome. Willitts. 1989. $40-50

40th Anniversary glitter dome. Willitts. 1990s. $50-60

TURN DOWN THAT MUSIC!

"Snoopy's Merry Christmas" LP record. Springboard International Records. 1978. $15-20

Shower radio. "Joe Cool Wet Tunes" by Salton. Early 1990s. $18-30

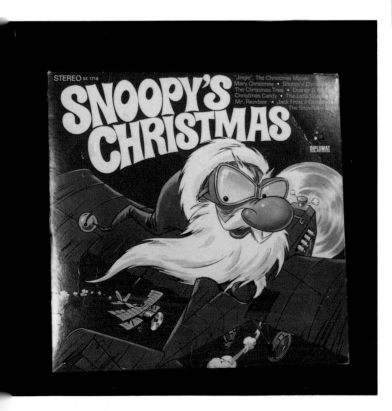

"Snoopy's Christmas" record. LP. Diplomat. 1970s. $15-20

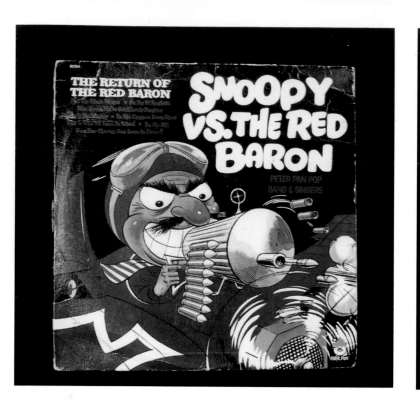

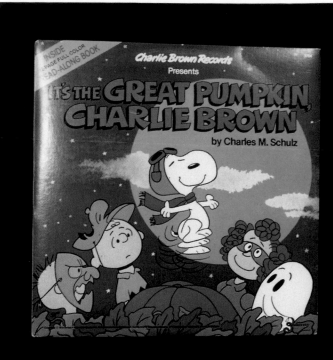

"Snoopy vs. the Red Baron" record. LP. Peter Pan Records. 1970s. $15-20

"It's the Great Pumpkin, Charlie Brown" record with book. LP. 1978. United Features Syndicate, Buena Vista Distribution. $15-20

"Snoopy and His Friends the Royal Guardsmen" record. 1970s. $12-15

"He's Your Dog, Charlie Brown" record. 33 RPM. 1978. $15-20

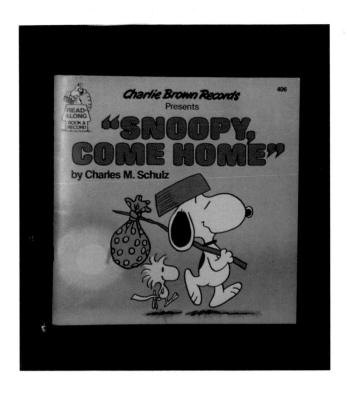

"Snoopy Come Home". Read along book. 45 RPM. 1980. $7-11

"Snoopy's Christmas" CDs and ornaments. Mid-1990s. $15-20

Compact disc ornaments from CEMA. 1993. $15-20

"Happy Anniversary Charlie Brown" and "Snoopy's Christmas," CDs. 1995. $15-17

ELECTRONIC SNOOPY

Snoopy plastic telephone. Determined Products. 1980s. $25-35

Joe Cool plastic telephone. Seika. 1990s.
$70-80

Plastic Snoopy and Woodstock telephone on woodgrain base.
American Telecommunications Corp. 1980s. $150-175

Wooden candlestick lamp. Snoopy and Woodstock glass globe.
Kamco. 1978. $65-85

Plastic and woodgrain Snoopy and Woodstock lamp and tele-phone. American Telecommunications Corp. 1980s. $150-200

Snoopy and Woodstock lamp with rainbow. Plastic. Nursery Originals, early 1980s. $60-75

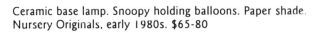

Ceramic base lamp. Snoopy holding balloons. Paper shade. Nursery Originals, early 1980s. $65-80

Ceramic lamp with Snoopy at typewriter. Metal shade. C.N. Burman. Early 1980s. $45-60

Ceramic sitting Snoopy night light. 1990.
Willitts. $20-30

Plastic light up Snoopy lamp. Bulb inside.
Gladys Goose Inc. 18". 1980. $60-75

Ceramic standing Snoopy lamp. C.N. Burman.
Early 1980s. $45-60

Lamp with Snoopy in tux next to lamp post.
Unknown manufacturer. $75-100

Snoopy catching butterflies, Japanese lantern. 1990s. $15-20

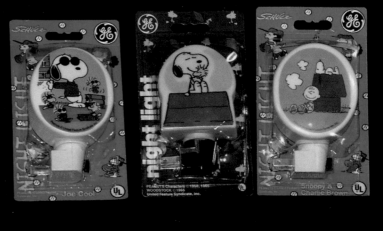

Plastic switch cover. 1980s. $6-8

Plastic light switch plates. Butterfly Co.,
Hallmark. Monogram Products,1980s.
$7-9 in package

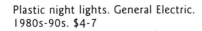

Plastic night lights. General Electric.
1980s-90s. $4-7

Plastic light switch plates. Hallmark. 1970s. $10-12 in package

Plastic light switch plate. Wecolite. 1980s-1990s. $5-7

Plastic light switch plates. 1980s. $6-8

Snoopy ice cream maker. Donvier. 1980s. $20-30

144

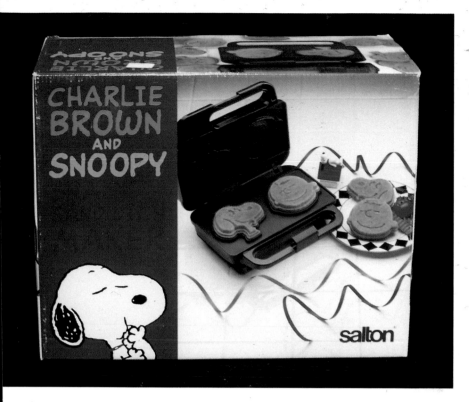

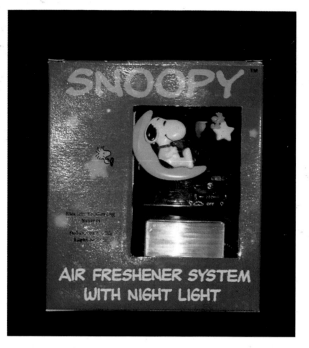

Plastic air freshener with night light. $25-35

Charlie Brown and Snoopy teflon sandwich
maker from Salton. 1990s. $30-45

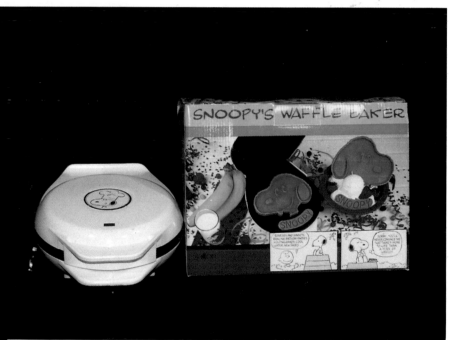

"Snoopy's Waffle Maker." Mid-1990s. Salton. $30-45.

Plastic hair dryer from Salton. Mid-1990s. $30-45

Metal alarm clock with Snoopy's arms as the clock hands. West Germany/Blessing/Determined Products. $25-35

Metal alarm clock. Snoopy dancing. Blessing/Determined. Early 1970s. 10". Came in different colors. $60-80

Metal alarm clock. Snoopy's arms move. Was available in many color combinations. Blessing/Determined. Early 1970s. 3.5" diameter. $35-45

Snoopy playing tennis, metal windup alarm clock from Equity. 4".
1980s. $50-65

Snoopy and Woodstock plastic battery operated alarm clock from
Equity. Early 1980s. $40-50 in box

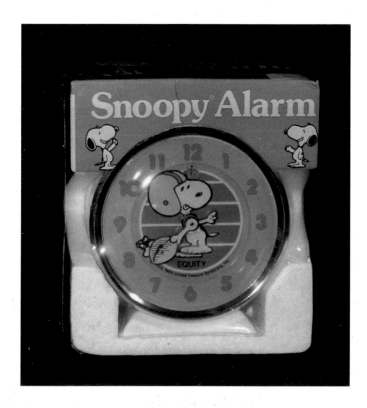

Football playing Snoopy, metal windup alarm clock from Equity. 4".
Early 1980s. $50-65

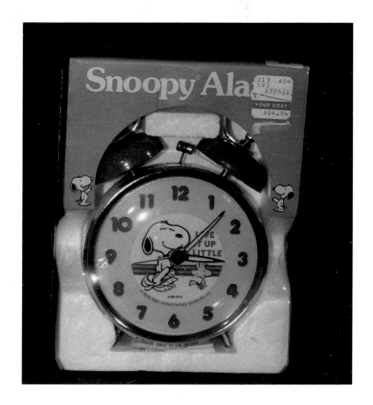

"Live It Up a Little," metal windup alarm clock from Equity. Early
1980s. 4". $50-65

Plastic clock from Citizen. 1980s. $20-30

Metal alarm clock. "I'm allergic to morning." 4". Equity. Early 1980s. $40-55

Metal alarm clock by Equity. Snoopy with checkered flag. Early 1980s. 4". $50-60

Snoopy with Woodstock alarm clock from Citizen, Japan. 1990s. $20-30

Plastic Snoopy wall clock. Citizen. Late 1980s. $30-40

Beagle Scout pendulum clock. Citizen, late 1980s. $45-55

Plastic Snoopy with Woodstock clock by
Citizen. 1980s. $20-30

Plush Snoopy with quartz analog alarm clock in belly. Armitron.
1990. $40-50

Joe Cool quartz alarm clock from Salton.
1990s. $20-25

Digital alarm clock. Snoopy's doghouse by Salton. 1990s. $20-25

Plastic quartz wall clock by Salton.
1990s. $18-25

Keywound alarm clock by Salton.
Metal and Plastic. 1990s. $15-20

Plastic Snoopy with Woodstock
clock. 1990s. $40-60

SNOOPY FINERY

CRYSTAL ANYONE?

Crystal Snoopy figurine. Determined. 1972.
$200-250

Crystal Snoopy from Sasaki Crystal. Japan.
1990s. $50-60

Crystal Snoopy paperweight from Sasaki
Crystal. Japan. 1990s. $50-60

Crystal Snoopy figurine. 21 mm. Silver Deer.
1990. $50-75

Crystal Snoopy literary Ace. Silver Deer. 1992.
$100-125

Crystal sitting Snoopy from Sasaki. 1990s.
$50-60

PRECIOUS METALS

Silverplate Snoopy bank. Baseball player. Leonard Silver. 1979.
$60-75

Silverplate heart-shaped box by Leonard Silver
Co. 1979. $30-40

Pewter Snoopy on train from Knott's Berry farms. 1990s.
$100-125

Pewter Snoopy letters forming train. 1990s. $200-225

Silverplate flower vase with Snoopy hanging on
edge. Leonard Silver. 1979. $30-40

Limited edition, solid bronze, sculpture set. Original art by Charles
Schulz. 1992. Each piece sits on engraved wood base and comes
in wooden box. Manufactured by International Trading Technol-
ogy. Designed by Stan Pawlowski. $750-900 set

Silverplate baby block bank by Leonard Silver Co. 3" x 3" x 3". 1979. $40-60 Also available but not shown. Snoopy sitting bank, $30-45

Silver plated Snoopy on dog house bank. Leonard Silver Co. 1979. 6.5". $30-45

Sitting Snoopy figurine, goldtone. Leonard. 1979. $30-40

Peanuts silverplated album frame with box. Godinger. Early 1990s. $30-40

Silverplated dresser set by Godinger. 1990. $30-40

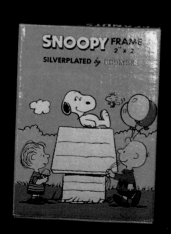

Silverplated Snoopy picture frame. Godinger. 1990. $15-25

Silverplated Snoopy doghouse bank by Godinger. Literary or Flying Ace. 1990. $20-25

Silverplated picture frame. Embossed dancing Snoopys on rim. Godinger. 1990. $20-25

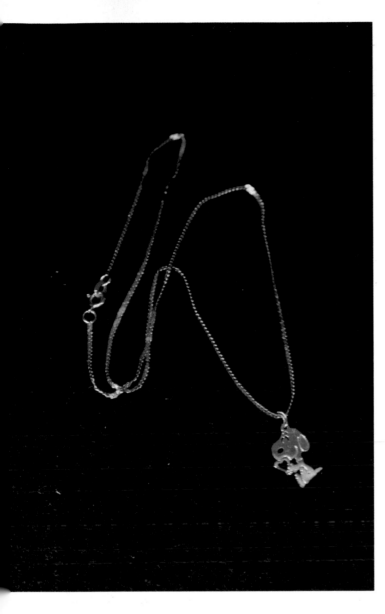

Gold Snoopy necklace. 1980s. $80-110

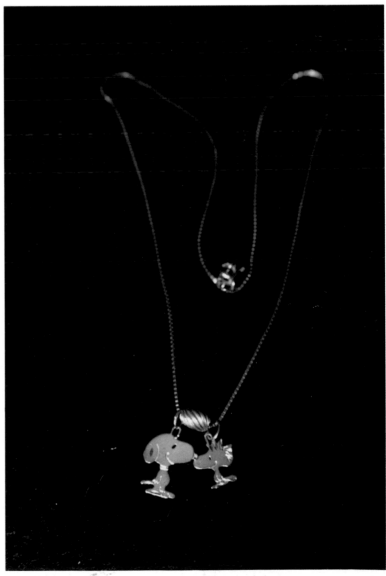

Brushed gold Snoopy and Woodstock necklace. Early 1990s.
$150-175

WHAT TIME IS IT?

45th anniversary metal watch from Armitron.
Glass dome with ceramic Snoopy on top.
1995. $60-75

Flying Ace metal watch
with leather band.
Armitron. Hands are
propellers. 1990. $80-100

Snoopy metalwatch with
leather band. Armitron.
1990. $80-100

Snoopy plastic watch with
plastic band. Armitron.
1990. $30-40

Snoopy metal watch with
leather band. Armitron.
1990s. $60-80

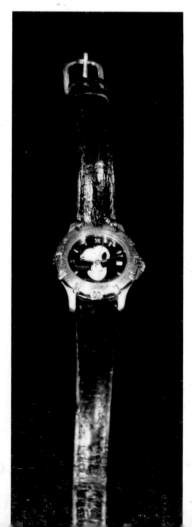

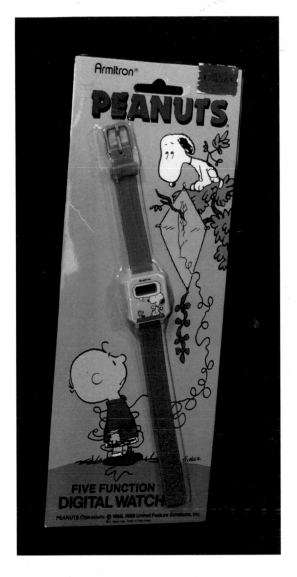

Peanuts five function digital watch from
Armitron. Late 1980s. Non replaceable battery.
$5-10

Goldtone and silvertone Snoopy pins. 1". 1990s. $10-12 each

JEWELRY FOR FUN

Goldtone Snoopy pin. 2". 1990s. $15-20

Metal enamel Snoopy earring holders. Late
1970s. $15-20

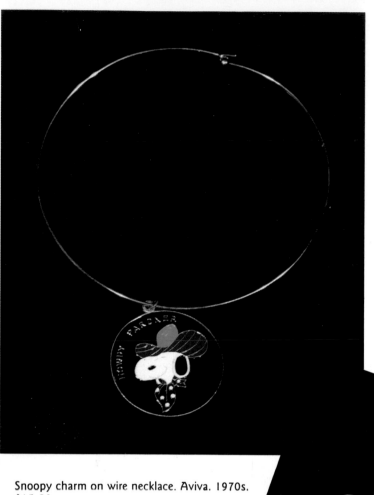

Goldtone earrings from Aviva. 1970s. $15-20 each

Snoopy charm on wire necklace. Aviva. 1970s. $15-20

Cloisonne pendant on chain from Aviva. 1970s. $10-15

Peanuts bracelet. Mid-1990s. $40-50

Gold tone character charm bracelet. Enamel. Aviva. 1965. $35-45

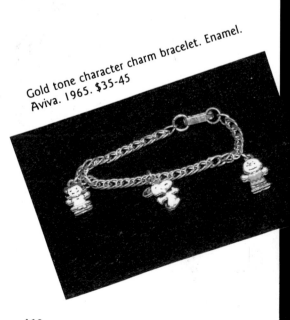

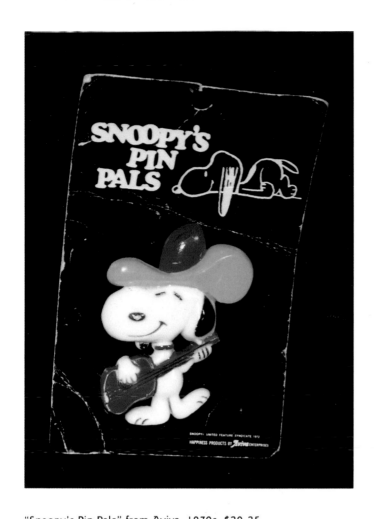

"Snoopy's Pin Pals" from Aviva. 1970s. $20-25

Snoopy cloisonne jewelry. 1970s. $20-30 set

Snoopy NFL Enamel pins, various teams.
1980s. Quantasia. $7-12

Peanuts 45th year anniversary pin. 1995. $4-6

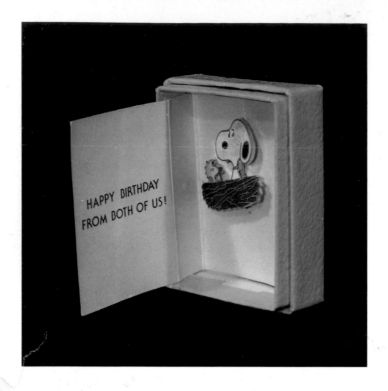

Snoopy surfing by Aviva Nifty Gifts. Came as enamel pin or earrings. Early 1970s. $15-20

Snoopy in nest with Woodstock by Aviva Nifty Gifts. Came as cloisonne pin or earrings. Early 1970s. $15-20

Dancing Snoopy by Aviva Nifty Gifts. Came as enamel pin or earrings. Early 1970s. $15-20

Snoopy lapel pins from Aviva. 1970s. $10-12 on card

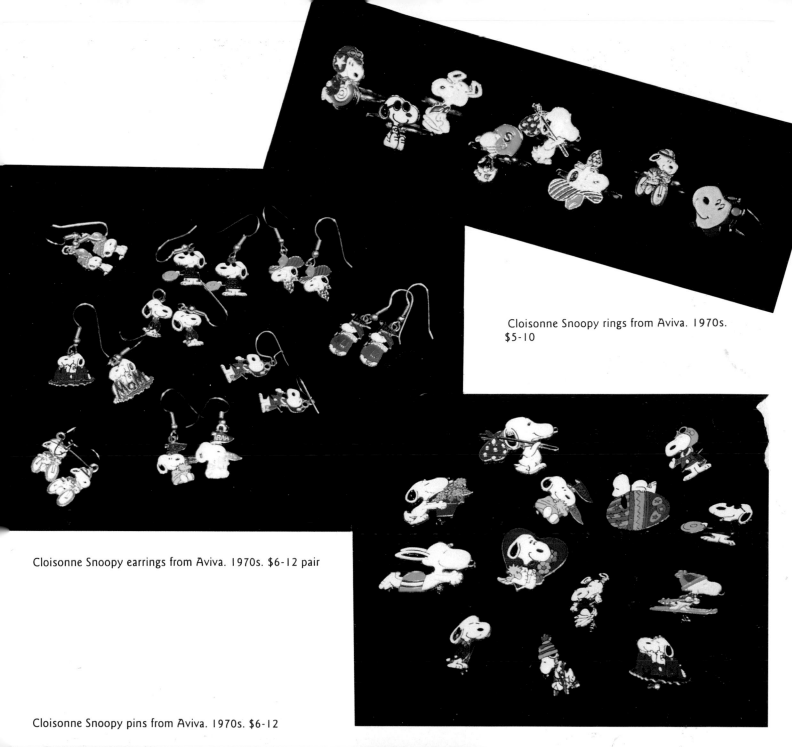

Cloisonne Snoopy rings from Aviva. 1970s. $5-10

Cloisonne Snoopy earrings from Aviva. 1970s. $6-12 pair

Cloisonne Snoopy pins from Aviva. 1970s. $6-12

Cloisonne Snoopy pins from Aviva. 1970s. $6-12 each

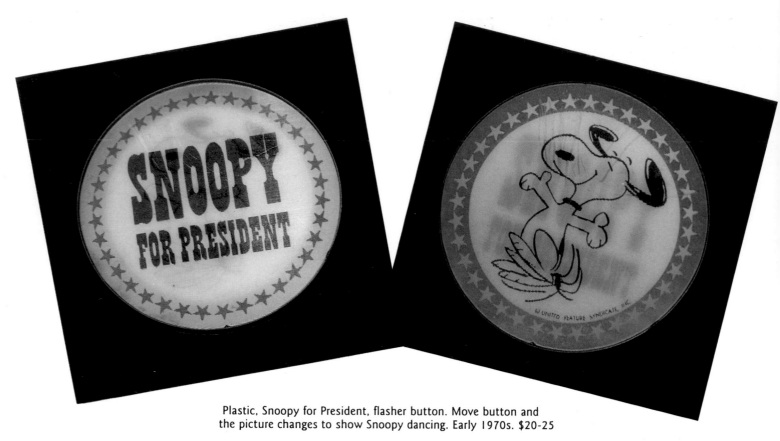

Plastic, Snoopy for President, flasher button. Move button and the picture changes to show Snoopy dancing. Early 1970s. $20-25

Pinbacks by Aviva. Plastic front metal back. Move button and the picture changes. 2.5". 1970s. $15-20.

Snoopy flasher campaign buttons. "Snoopy for President" flashes to dancing Snooping. Plastic. Hallmark. Early 1990s. $20-25. With display $175-200. Button on bottom of house display. Simon Simple. 1972. Metal 2.5". $20-25. Also available 1.5" and 0.5" $12-15 each

Pinback with Snoopy and birds from Simon
Simple. 1.75". Early 1970s. $15-20

Snoopy and Woodstock pinback. Simon Simple.
Early 1970s. 6". $25-35

12 pinbacks. Metal 1.5" each sold seperately.
Early 1970s. Simon Simple. $20-25 each

Metal pinback. 1.75". Early 1970s. Simon
Simple. $15-20

"Snoopy for President" pin. 1970s. $10-12

"Knott's Camp Snoopy" pin. 1990s. $3-5

"Snoopy Fan Club" pin. 1980s. $4-8

Snoopy pin. "Love Me." 1980s. $4-6

Plastic "Blarney Beagle" pin. 1980s. $5-6

SPECIAL STUFF

Cotton "Apollo 11 Lunar Team" patch. 25th Anniversary. $60-80

Camp Snoopy collectors coins from Knott's Berry Farm. Grand Opening of Camp Snoopy in Bloomington, Minnesota. Nickel silver. 1992. $6-10

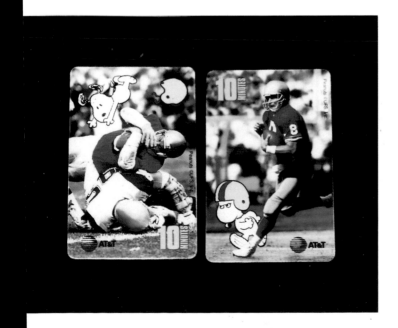

Plastic phone cards. Steve Young from San Francisco 49ers. Made by ATT. "Snoopy Bowl." 1995. $10-12 each

Coins of the Presidents book. 1970s. Snoopy's penny coin collection book. Jerry Briskin Enterprises. $25-35 each

ADVERTISING WITH OUR FAVORITE BEAGLE!

Metlife began advertising with Snoopy as early as 1987.

Advertising poster from Metlife. Early 1990s. (Sent out free when requested). $4-5

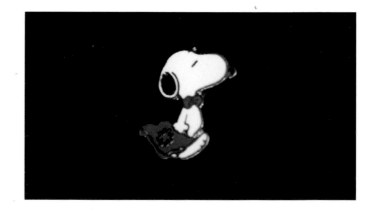

Metlife advertising pin. 1980s/90s. $10-15

Cardboard Metlife advertising. 5 feet tall. Mid-1990s. $50-75

Advertising playing cards from Metlife. 1990s. $10-12

Advertising kite from Metlife. This was a free
promotional kite. 1990s. $2-3

Plastic frisbies from Metlife. 1990s. $5-7

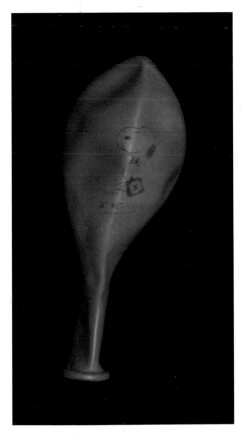

Advertising balloon from Metlife.
1990s. $1-2

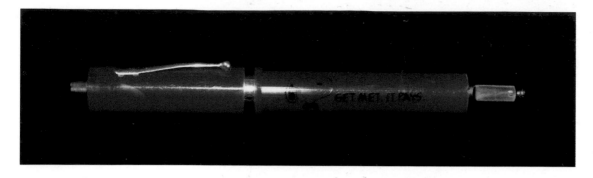

Advertising pen from Metlife. 1990s. $6-8

Ceramic advertising cups from Metlife. 1990s. $10-15 each

Advertising plastic ice scraper from Metlife.
1980s/1990s. $7-10

Plastic covered mug from
Metlife. 1980s/1990s. $6-8

Nylon Brock-a-brella from Metlife. 1980s. $12-15

Fabric carry-all from Metlife. St. Louis Cardinals logo. $10-15 mint

Fabric carry-all from Metlife. Throughout the late 1980s/1990s
Metlife sponsored many sports events with wonderful totebags.
$10-15 mint

Plastic and metal advertising key chain from Metlife. 1990s. $6-10

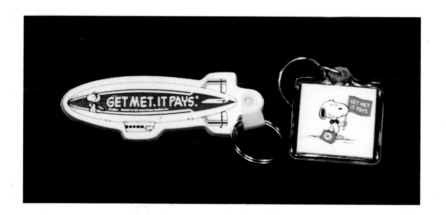

Advertising key chains from Metlife. 1980s/1990s. $6-8

"A Family's Guide to Child Safety" Metlife.
(Was sent out free when requested). 1990s.
$1-2

"Chex Party Mix" advertising label. 1990s. $1-2

uggage tag from Metlife. 1990s. $4-6

A&W began advertising with Snoopy as early as 1989 and continued only through 1994.

Cardboard advertising banner from A & W rootbeer. 6' long 12" deep. 1990s. $2-3

Aluminum 6 pack cans of Snoopy soda from A & W root beer. Early to mid-1990s. Came in Cream soda and in regular or diet. 6 pack-full. $5-8

Plastic cups from A & W rootbeer. 1990s. $12-15 set

Snoopy video tank topper advertising for Shell Oil. 1993. $7-10

Cardboard banner from card display. Hallmark. 1970s. $10-15

Snoopy in Uncle Sam top hat. Interstate Brands (Dolly Madison, Weber's Bread, Butternut, Mrs. Karl's). Four shrink wrapped posters include other characters. Promotional. 1970s. $25-40 set

174

Snoopy for President pin. 1970s. $10-12

Snoopy's gallery and gift shop pin. 1980s. $4-6

Advertising round sticker for Snoopy Shoes.
1970s. $3-4

Snoopy for President pin. $8-10

Advertising from Fox River Mall. Mid-1990s. $1-2

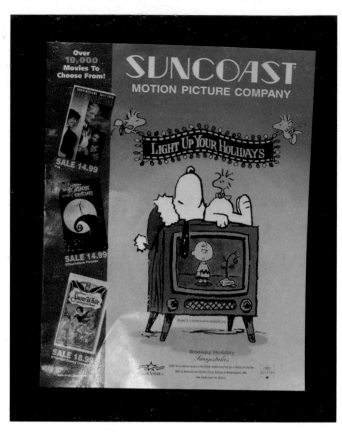

Suncoast Christmas ad. 1994. $1-2

Advertising from National Golf Federation. Golf
course etiquette. 1995. $1-2

Snoopy decals from Dolly Madison.
1980s. $5-7

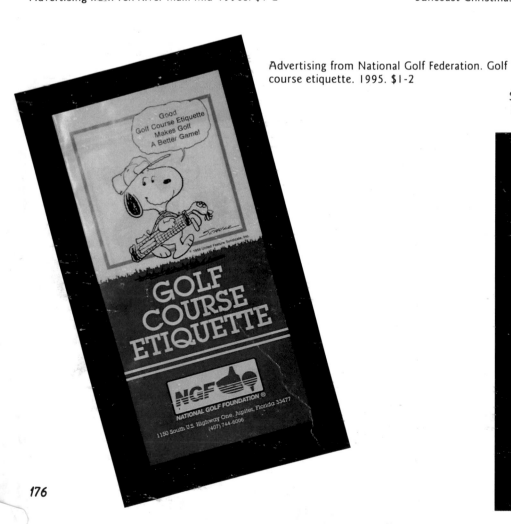

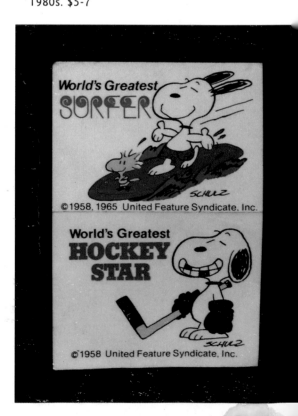